Surviving and Succeeding in Difficult Classrooms

Second edition

Paul Blum

Routledge
Taylor & Francis Group

LONDON AND NEW YORK

First published 1998
by Routledge

Second edition published 2006
by Routledge
2 Park Square, Milton Park, Abingdon, Oxon OX14 4RN

Simultaneously published in the USA and Canada
by Routledge
270 Madison Ave, New York, NY 10016

Routledge is an imprint of the Taylor & Francis Group, an informa business

Typeset in Palatino by
Newgen Imaging Systems (P) Ltd, Chennai, India
Printed and bound in Great Britain by
TJ International Ltd, Padstow, Cornwall

British Library Cataloguing in Publication Data
A catalogue record for this book is available from
the British Library

Library of Congress Cataloging in Publication Data
Blum, Paul.
    Surviving and succeeding in difficult classrooms / Paul Blum. –
2nd ed.
      p.cm.
    1. Problem children–Education (Secondary)–Great Britain. 2. High
school teaching–Great Britain. 3. Classroom management–Great
Britain. I. Title.

LC4803.G7B58 2006
371.930941–dc22   2005029801

ISBN10: 0–415–39720–0
ISBN13: 978–0–415–39720–9

Surviving and Succeeding in Difficult Classrooms

In its second edition, this book brings us up-to-date with what it is like to be a teacher in a difficult class, and regularly faced with apathy, defiance and aggression.

Sadly, numerous government initiatives since the 1998 publication of the first edition of this bestselling text have not transformed the situation for teachers in difficult classrooms. Here, Paul Blum explores the impact and consequences of the changes made in the intervening years.

Substantially revised, *Surviving and Succeeding in Difficult Classrooms* now includes sections on teaching pupils with low reading ages, and on making the most effective use of teaching assistants.

Like its predecessor it offers sensible, practical advice, for all classroom teachers, on how to survive and succeed in the face of tremendous difficulty.

Paul Blum has spent 20 years working at all levels from classroom teacher to deputy head in secondary schools in London.

This book was written in the author's free time and the views expressed represent the views of the author – they are not based on any particular school, and do not represent th

Related titles from Routledge

*A Teacher's Guide to Anger
Management*
Paul Blum
0–415–23198–1

*Surviving and Succeeding in
Senior School Management:
Getting in and getting on*
Paul Blum
0–415–39259–4 (hb)
0–415–39260–8 (pb)

*Improving Low Reading Ages
in the Secondary School:
Practical strategies for learning support*
Paul Blum
0–415–32909–4

*The A–Z of Learning: Tips
and Techniques for Teachers*
Mike Leibling and
Robin Prior
0–415–33506–X

Teacher Well-Being
Elizabeth Holmes
0–415–33498–5

*Professional Standards for
Teachers and School Leaders:
A key to school improvement*
Edited by Howard Green
0–415–33528–0

*Stress Relief for Teachers: The
coping triangle*
Claire Hayes
0–415–36933–9 (hb)
0–415–36934–7 (pb)

In memory of Aleksander Blum (1908–1996)

Contents

Acknowledgements

I am grateful for the comments of Nick Williams and the invaluable help and advice of Valerie Coultas, a skilled and inspirational inner-city teacher. I am grateful too for the brilliant, practical examples of Harry Peck as a Head of Year, who sadly is no longer alive.

Thanks also to the philosophical lead of Peter Searl. Although I was reluctant to accept his ideas at the time, I have learnt, with experience, that his compassion was entirely appropriate. Finally, thanks to Suzie Lloyd and Marie Healey whose 'infectious' humour helped many teachers struggle on and make sense of the topsy-turvy world of education on the front line.

Paul Blum
London, December 1997

Introduction

Since I first wrote this book back in 1997, there have been a number of attempts to change the teaching and learning experiences in secondary schools – especially challenging ones. There have been new Ofsted inspection guide lines; changes to the types of exams on offer with increased emphasis on vocational qualification; major government strategies to challenge the way that schools manage behaviour through the policy of Inclusion as well as major initiatives to raise standards in literacy and numeracy in the first three years of secondary schooling. We have moved into an era where schools are not only compared by their actual exam results but also by value added data. As I write, teachers are about to enter a work force agreement which should give them more time to prepare lessons and mark work. There is an ever increasing amount of staff in schools to work on clerical and administrative tasks and substitute for some aspects of teachers' work, as learning support assistants. The teaching profession itself has undergone a number of pay and condition changes with higher salaries for experienced teachers. More teachers than ever have become part of the senior school leadership structure. The Government has set up city academies in challenging urban areas and is allowing sponsors from private enterprise to run these new look schools. It has given them the authority to deviate from the national curriculum.

And yet the problems I described in 1997 are still prevalent in difficult classrooms, eight years on. Recent fly on the wall programmes filmed secretly by teachers on supply contract in difficult urban schools show staff still face the issues that I am about to describe. If anything, they may have got slightly worse as the policy to include ever more children with severe behaviour difficulties in main stream classes and not special schools, has added a further dimension to levels of disruption.

EDUCATIONAL CHANGE IN THE LAST DECADE AND ITS IMPACT ON DIFFICULT CLASSROOMS

There have been a variety of attempts to get to grips with the problems of literacy and numeracy that underpin a lot of the problems of disaffected school pupils. The National Literacy and Numeracy Strategies have been in force for the the last five years. The initiative was extended out of the numeracy and literacy hours of the primary schools. It may have made a marginal improvement on pupils at the top or middle end of the spectrum but there are still at least 20 per cent of pupils (mainly boys) coming in to secondary school with reading ages of a nine year old or less, when they are eleven. Where these intakes are heavily concentrated (up to half a Year 7 intake) – the classrooms remain restless and concentration/motivation poor. The Strategies have not touched this bottom end, where literacy recovery is still the key issue. As secondary school teachers in difficult classrooms you will still have to beg, steal or borrow good teaching materials and colourful ideas to make tough lessons work. We will look at an emergency tool kit for supporting low literacy levels in Chapter 3.

The logic of behaviour policy on Inclusion is that pupils with learning difficulties will develop better self esteem if they are taught alongside their mainstream peers. When this is well resourced, it has been very positive for pupils with various physical difficulties. But the inclusion of more pupils with severely challenging behaviour, has made even more difficult for ordinary teachers to control their classes.

Schools have increasingly set up their own Inclusion Units (Special Schools within Schools) to try and contain this extreme minority. This has sometimes helped to relieve the pressure on mainstream teachers by giving their lessons some respite from the most volatile characters. But the Units are unable to fulfil a central philosophy of Inclusion, which states they should only be a temporary intervention to help pupils sort out their behaviour, before going on back into the mainstream. Only a tiny minority of pupils ever return to their ordinary classes, sufficiently 'cured' of their disruptive behaviour. Most cannot leave the security of the Inclusion Unit.

The Blair Government have made some attempt to soften the blow of League tables, which show schools ranked by exam results. They have introduced an element of value added, so that school with challenging student populations can show improvements from the relatively low bases on which they are starting. But whilst it is good to celebrate the progress that can be made in tough schools, it doesn't change the actual daily struggle that the teachers face in the classroom.

'Value Added' has gone through the roof for some schools as some wily head teachers have realised that some vocational qualifications can be counted as the equivalent of four GCSEs. Consequently, results in some challenging schools have rocketed up from 20 per cent to 70 per cent of pupils gaining an equivalent of 5 A to C. But even when these schools have transformed grades, the teachers still face a daily battle in many difficult classrooms.

What has remained a disturbing constant in the last eight years is the political rhetoric condemning classrooms in difficult schools. Even as I write this chapter revision, an education secretary has announced that failure will not be tolerated and a school deemed to be failing could be shut within just one year. This kind of sabre rattling at schools facing difficulties, has been a common feature of the last decade with promised 'fresh start' schools, being put forward as a panacea for improving education in tough classrooms. As most of the transformation schemes are unrealistic, they soon fizzle out, but the threat of punishment for failure keeps the tension levels in difficult schools very high and adds stress, to what is already a challenging job.

FOR WHOM IS THIS BOOK INTENDED?

This book is meant to help classroom teachers with practical tips for handling difficult groups of students and difficult situations in their schools. There will often be situations in which they are faced with defiance, aggression and verbal and physical abuse. The advice will also include dealing with low-level energy-sapping daily routines in which they struggle to get the pupils to stop talking and actually listen to what they are saying.

Practical advice given here about surviving and succeeding in stressful and draining environments presented by the truly difficult secondary school would also be useful for teachers who have many positive teaching experiences during a normal week but also encounter some of the 'wild' and 'unruly' school situations which are the norm in rough schools.

The first and important lesson for any teacher in a tough secondary school is to get your overall thinking right, therefore a lot of current management jargon about improvement through target setting, action planning and constant monitoring must be discounted. The Ofsted criteria for transforming the difficult schools of the country will not help you make sense of the daily turmoil of your experience in a rough school. You must find your own practical way of achieving something that is educationally positive. So start by disregarding the ever prevailing Inspector and School Management positions, which say that pupils behave badly when the quality of teaching is insufficiently stimulating. They often behave badly when lessons are brilliantly planned because they prevent the teacher from starting properly; they often behave badly because they have poor skills in the subject areas they are being asked to study (usually literacy and numeracy); but, most importantly, they often behave badly because they have a very thin layer of motivation and a low level of concentration. The Inspectors say they have identified some teachers who are capable of functioning more effectively than others in very difficult classrooms, but do not be demoralised by this statement. The vast majority of teachers would, and do, struggle when faced with large numbers of poorly motivated and badly behaved pupils.

Some schools are told they are failing and are put onto 'Special Measures'. Some schools pass their Ofsted inspections and are deemed to be giving 'value for money', whatever that means. But the actual differences between the difficult school that passes and the one that fails is probably much smaller than you think. Both will have huge numbers of problem classes and plenty of unruly behaviour. The 'successful' one will have made a good case to the Inspectors that they have management systems for continually trying to improve the situation, the 'failed' one will not. What this works out as in practice is that the 'bad schools' are the difficult schools with poorly motivated intakes and 'good' schools are the ones with motivated intakes and what lies between has a mixture of both and are therefore neither 'good' or 'bad' schools. A fairer definition of a 'good school' is one in which the staff are pulling together as a team with shared educational objectives to make a real difference to pupils they teach

A good school could be one with an extremely difficult intake but where the staff use tremendous dedication and energy to give the pupils who want to learn a stable environment to do it in. Yet this institution may be deemed as 'failing' because it is outside the Ofsted Inspectors statistical safety net of 70 per cent of lessons 'satisfactory' or better, 90 per cent attendance and 20 per cent 'five A to C grade' passes at GCSE. Yet a nearby school with sluggish teaching, unimaginative educational management, and a stale culture which eschews change, could be safely exceeding the baseline statistics because of its highly motivated pupil intake and supportive parents. Which is the 'good' school and which is the 'bad'? Therefore, to survive in a difficult school you must be aware of these basic truths. You can only survive and succeed if you reject the labels of bad school and bad teacher. Remember a few simple facts. How many teachers who are judged 'excellent' in grammar schools would be able to teach effectively in a tough inner city school? How many Inspectors, who were once teachers, would be able to pick up your chalk and do the things they are telling you to do better? Writing a development plan is much easier than putting it into practice with an unruly class on a Friday afternoon.

INSPECTIONS AND Ofsted: MAKING SENSE OF IT

Not all the Ofsted Inspectorate's suggestions should be completely dismissed if you are in a difficult school. Their clinical inspection technique has potential advantages as well as drawbacks. A lot of the information it produces is judgemental in an unhelpful and unrealistic way, but some of it can be helpful to you and your school if used intelligently. Recent changes to the inspection system encourage schools to use self-evaluation to work out what their own strong and weak points are. This is a welcome development along with the promise of shorter 'lighter touch' inspections from 2005 onwards.

Bad things

The Ofsted teams inspect with the criteria of a 'satisfactory' national norm in their heads. Schools that have many difficult classes will measure at a deviation well below that.

The teaching and learning in their classrooms will be labelled 'poor', 'borderline' or 'unsatisfactory', using the Ofsted criteria, even when a teacher has sweated blood to contain and then turn round difficulties during a lesson.

But the Inspectors have little interest in whether a lesson is 'good' in the context of a difficult group of individuals in a 'rough' school; they are more concerned with whether it is 'good' in national terms. A lesson in an inner-city school is judged on exactly the same criteria as a lesson at a grammar school. The social, political and economic contexts of the schools is briefly written about in the introduction to an Ofsted report, and ignored thereafter. Lesson grading is standardised against all the country's schools.

So if you have a restless and poorly motivated class, you've had it! You will be graded at below satisfactory or poor, even if you battle and manage to control the group so that they have stopped climbing up the window sills and are all working. Inspectors don't usually spend much more than twenty minutes in any one lesson as they feverishly try to clock up a regulation sample of observations.

They are unlikely to remain long enough to see you turn a lesson round, or they will arrive too late to see how well you managed to start the lesson. Their fatally flawed assumption is to take good behaviour and responsiveness to the learning opportunity as a normal prerequisite for all pupils.

This may be the norm in some schools but it is 'abnormally good going' in many others and very difficult to achieve.

Acceptable behaviour and motivation, as we shall see in this book, is something than cannot be taken for granted in many schools – it is the central struggle of each lesson. Much more praiseworthy credit should be given where it is obviously difficult to achieve. Yet the Ofsted Inspectors have a tendency to demoralise teachers by condemning them and the lesson as 'poor' if they have struggled to control badly behaved pupils.

Don't let the propaganda demoralise you. If you are the kind of person who can 'survive' and get some effective airspace in which pupils listen to you in a difficult school, you are already an effective and tenacious teacher.

In an easier setting you would be 'excellent'.

Good things

Inspections can nevertheless be useful. The clinical objectivity that leads to norm referencing can be used productively when applied to identifying the problems facing a 'difficult' school. Inspections can identify whole school strengths and weaknesses in a fresh way because they are independent observers on a short stay. Their looking glass reveals a 'true reflection'. They often point out issues that a school has missed seeing for itself, although they have been perched on the end of the school's nose. For example:

- What makes some classroom practice 'excellent' in certain areas?
- Why are so many pupils late for their lessons?
- Why is there such as a lack of common approach to literacy, numeracy and assessment? If the information is then used intelligently by the internal management of the institution, it can help improve the lot of an ordinary classroom teacher.

WHAT IS A 'DIFFICULT' SECONDARY SCHOOL?

It is not the purpose of this book to go into long definitions. This is a simple guide. A 'difficult' secondary school is:

- a school which is bottom or near the bottom of the examinations league table in its local area;
- a school which is likely to get between 0 and 25 per cent of pupils achieving 'five A to C passes' at GCSE;
- a school which has to struggle to keep attendance in the mid-80 per cent bracket and unauthorised absence to under 5 per cent, without cheating;
- a school in which about 40 per cent or more pupils have free school meals;
- a school with a high number of pupils with language and literacy difficulties;
- a school forced to take a large casual intake (often excluded from the local more popular schools or locally disbanded Special Schools) because it is undersubscribed.

Some or all of these factors will be in operation in the most challenging schools. As these factors diminish, the practical measures that I describe to deal with incidents will also dilute them.

Varying 'difficulties' in different schools

My general argument is that 'difficult' schools and 'difficult classes' throw up a very similar range of problems, but there are some regional or local varieties that add to the flavour of an individual school's difficulties.

1 Recent immigration – where a refugee intake to a school lives in temporary housing and bed and breakfast.

These newly arrived populations move around and often do not speak English. As a teacher you can be faced with a room full of pupils who, while you are trying to teach them, are chatting in a language you do not understand. In these circumstances, control and communication are very difficult. Contacting home also becomes a problem.

2 Communities with very high unemployment, especially among young people. This, understandably, often creates a great degree of cynicism among your clients about the value of education. It also leads to high level of truancy and parental condonement.

3 Schools where the strongly held moral or religious beliefs of a vociferous minority among the parents, or on the governing body, lead to a clash between sections of pupils, parents, teachers and governors or a whole mixture at the same time.

4 Schools which serve specific local communities in which there are already serious rivalries or tensions of clan, religion, race or extended family feud. This brings gangs to the school gates or into school and will cause chaos.

Part I

The learning experience in your classroom

Chapter 1

Purposeful lessons

THE INGREDIENTS FOR A PURPOSEFUL LESSON

To create an effective learning experience in any classroom (whatever the school) the teacher has to be able to create a purposeful and calm atmosphere in which the momentum for learning can be built. The observer of an effective lesson will often describe a situation in which the teacher establishes high expectations of the pupils and sets up an agenda which challenges them. The best lessons have pace and rigour, which is just another way of saying they have good natural momentum.

This is easily achieved when the pupils have a strong degree of internal self-motivation. When they are asked to listen or respond to each other and the teacher, they do so willingly and enthusiastically. They are prepared to cooperate with the dynamic set up by their teacher. They adapt smoothly to established routines of not shouting out, and not interrupting the answers of the teacher or the other pupils. They stay in their seats, do not arrive late for lessons, can work in groups, etc.

In a difficult school absolutely none of this can be taken for granted, however experienced the teacher may be.

There are a number of serious hurdles to be cleared before learning of any sort can begin.

A learning momentum is self-generating in a well-motivated class. Pupils give useful input to the teacher who can use it to build the learning experience organically. In a difficult class, the teacher has to provide most of the input and structure to the lesson. The lesson has to be planned very carefully, and the behaviour of the pupils managed impeccably, before any useful class response can be exploited and purposely fed back into the lesson.

TEACHER SURVEY

In how many of your classes this week have students exhibited the characteristics displayed in this guide? Use this checklist and grade your lessons against it.

A This type of behaviour never occurs in my lessons.
B This type of behaviour occasionally occurs in a few of my lessons.
C This type of behaviour occurs regularly in a few of my lessons.
D This type of behaviour is often displayed in my lessons.
E This type of behaviour and worse is displayed in most of my lessons.

1 Students won't come into the room at the beginning of the lesson, take their coats off and sit down in a seat, without major interventions from the teacher (wasting at least 5 minutes of lesson time).
2 Small groups of students arrive late. They come in and immediately start talking to the class that you've been trying to settle. The whole process of sitting them down, giving out exercise books and getting coats off, has to begin again.

3 While you are trying to begin the lessons, students will continue conversations which are very difficult to stop. This could be aggravated by their sitting half or fully turned away from you.

4 Students will get out of their seats without asking permission and go to talk to or interfere with others in the room.

5 Students will shout across the room, get out of their seats, hit other pupils or take their possessions. These students will often run in and out of the room, taking no notice of your instructions.

6 Students will start talking to their neighbours as soon as you start to address the class or ask a question.

7 Students will shout out answers, or shout out comments or questions over your speech, which will spoil the momentum of your teaching. They often have nothing to do with the 'concepts' you are trying to develop.

8 Students will argue and insult each other and this could lead at worst to a fight and at best to another round of heated quarrelling.

9 Students bristle aggressively if asked to stop talking or interrupting the flow of the lesson. This is likely to get into a verbal confrontation if your requests to stop interrupting persist. Trying to move them from their friendship groups is certain to lead to 'refusal' and open outright confrontation.

10 Students tear up their worksheets and throw the pieces on the floor or use the sheets to make darts or pellets to flick at other members of the class, or you. They flick ink and scribble over exercise books and textbooks. They send notes to each other on paper torn out of exercise books or folders.

11 Students eat sweets, crisps and chew gum all through the lesson. They discard wrappings on the floor or throw them in the general direction of the bin, where they pile up on the floor.

12 Students write no more than a few lines during the lesson, certainly a lot less than they are capable of. Some are likely to ignore your instructions to hand books in or take them home. The books will be left on the desk or the floor as pupils make a hasty exit for their next inter-lesson rendezvous.

13 As the end of the lesson approaches, pupils will start putting their coats on and packing their bags before you have asked them to. They will get out of their seats before the signal for the end of class and will walk around the room or out of it. You use a lot of energy trying to persuade them to return to their seats.

14 There is a general feeling of restlessness and 'movement' in the room from the moment your lesson starts. Pupils fidget or loll in their chairs. They are so busy talking to each other that they find it difficult to focus on you.

15 Even worse, in some lessons – especially those before lunch or in the afternoon – there is an overall feeling that can only be described as a 'semi-frenzy'. People are falling out of their chairs, shouting at each other and at no one in particular, laughing and screaming as if drunk or hysterical. They are prone to abusing each other and starting a play or real fight. When you talk personally to individuals in a quiet voice, they shout back their reply. Speaking to them is almost impossible.

If you have scored A on all the above, you probably won't find this book useful but if you have scored any other grade, B to E, on any other combination of statements, you can get some handy tips from this survival guide. Even if you have only scored B to E on statement 5, 6 or 14, this book could be very useful.

TEACHING THE LESSONS: FACING THE REALITY OF THE CLASSROOM

Very few teachers in difficult schools can put a complete stop to all of the above characteristics during their lessons. A few exceptional individuals don't experience these problems. They are often charismatic bullies with the main emphasis on the second word, and therefore their actual style is difficult to copy and best avoided, as they thrive on the reinforcement of the negative and the aggressive stereotypes that the local community condones but local school is seeking to challenge. There is also another rare combination of the brilliantly inspirational and incredibly well-organised teachers, following up every tiny misdemeanour so that they break the few that would resist their incredible teaching. Each quality is rare in the majority of teachers and the second without the first would be the recipe for stress, confrontation and nervous breakdown as there are countless things in any day to challenge and punish. Most teachers fall into the middle – they do not wish to and cannot bludgeon and bully the pupils into submission. They are not inspirational or relentless enough to squash all challenges to their attempts to teach and they become angry, frustrated and demoralised by all the hassle. They have to rely on a mixture of strategies to survive and succeed.

Contrary to increasing voiced school-improvement theory and Ofsted myth, good teachers and good teaching materials will not extinguish bad behaviour of the kind listed in the fifteen points. Bad behaviour is not simply a by-product of bad teaching which lacks pace and rigour. You must not allow these much-voiced doctrines to grind down your self-esteem as a teacher in a difficult school. Bad behaviour is inextricably interlinked with poor pupil motivation towards the process of learning at school.

Brilliant teaching will usually contrast indifferent or poor teaching but nothing is going to turn a class of nutters into a class of angels. Good teaching strategies and expertly planned lessons can be steamrollered by very poorly motivated pupils.

You will survive and succeed in a difficult school if you are steadfastly enthusiastic, plan carefully and communicate colourfully when you get the chance. You must try to stay calm in the face of constant provocation and confrontation. In lessons, you must pursue positive behaviour management strategies energetically to create the artificial student motivation that is so often lacking. You must not allow yourself to become completely frustrated by expecting too much of the pupils, nor must you accept the bare minimum that they offer – and avoid challenging them. Instead, you must stay calm, be positive and make small steps towards progress. This is not an easy path!

The context

The biggest problem that must be faced by a teacher in a difficult school is that there is a substantial minority of pupils who have no profound interest in studying the current curriculum on offer. Their parents are not going to give you effective support with these adolescents because they themselves were not too motivated towards studying a similar curriculum twenty years ago.

Neither parents nor children have particular skills or knowledge that would help them succeed with the academic diet on offer. There is also a smaller minority of pupils (between 1 and 15 in any single class) who are completely dysfunctional and will disturb your lessons, and those of almost everyone else, for a variety of reasons – all of which are beyond your reasonable control.

Schools offer a strange context for effective learning and teaching to take place. They are the only educational institutions in this country which you have to attend up to a certain age, irrespective of whether you are inclined to learn anything or not. All colleges, universities and other forms of training rely on people being there because they want to and leaving if they do not. All these other institutions would ask people to leave if they were impeding the process of learning for others in the group by their disaffected behaviour. But teachers in a difficult school have to put up with rudeness and interruptions every lesson, with only the grossest forms of behaviour leading ultimately to permanent pupil exclusion.

The best learning situations are those in which the receivers of knowledge are trying as hard as they can to take on knowledge and skills. The activity is purely voluntary, which is why it works so well. But many difficult schools are more like a prison or an army barracks in which many unwilling people are being asked to do compulsory national service. This element of compulsion poisons the ideal learning situation. The ordinary teacher has to make the best of this very difficult reality. He or she has to get the best out of the well-motivated pupil while trying to tame or calm others who are behaving like 'caged animals' in a zoo.

Your biggest challenge is to get pupils into the mood to listen and then work.

MOTIVATION: STRATEGIES FOR CREATING IT

Positive behaviour management

Ideally this should be operated in all schools. Everyone should do much the same thing in the same situations, which would dramatically impact on behaviour and motivation. But the bleak reality in schools which have countless behavioural breaches is that you, the teacher, will have to fight for control in your own classroom, using your own style and your own positive behavioural systems. Much of what you do will form your own personal crusade to survive. You must ask for help but do so sparingly as your senior colleagues are inundated with continual fire-fighting. (See later Chapters.)

The most difficult thing to do is to think positively when everything around you would appear to be frustratingly negative. What the teacher sees is a classroom full of pupils talking and shouting abuse at each other, perhaps leaving their seats to interfere with others. Each time you struggle to gain their attention, a steady trickle of late-comers disturb the room again. You find yourself arguing with countless pupils about taking off their coats, chewing gum during your lesson and chatting instead of listening to you. Yet the more negative and frustrating the situation, the more vital is the need to positively reward those who are doing what you want. The more you scan your own room for positive signs from the students, the more you will realise that what is going wrong is persistently represented by a minority. The vast majority are often ready and waiting for you to begin your lesson, but can become bored and frustrated doing so.

Therefore, rewarding the positive near the start of a difficult lesson is vital. The longer the lesson takes to get into gear, the harder it becomes to pull it back into equilibrium. An upward spiral needs to be created with the majority of the class feeling they are progressing and doing something constructive. This is critical to your success and survival.

The smiley face stamp

Business travellers would not leave on a foreign trip without their charge cards and I wouldn't enter a classroom of a difficult school without my smiley face stamp. It is a small ink stamp, easily obtainable from most shops and education catalogues for a couple of pounds. It makes a happy red face on a pupil's written work.

If you are struggling with a difficult class, I advise the liberal use of the smiley face in the first critical ten minutes of a lesson. Its most important use is to galvanise the attention of the majority of the class at that critical time when they are largely ignoring you and talking among themselves. The stamp can kick start the lesson. It can be offered to those who start listening and put up their hands to answer your questions. It can be used to reward those who are sitting down, have removed their coats and are waiting for the lesson to begin. The objective is to get, on the board, a long list of names of pupils who are doing things that you need done. Their names can be scribbled quickly and the stamp put on their books in a calmer part of the lesson. This will have a double benefit of positive reinforcement, just as you want them to start written work.

So what real worth does a smiley face stamp have on a pupil's book? To many pupils it would not matter if it had no legitimate currency in a school reward system outside of your classroom. They respond positively to the immediate gratification of having their own positive action recognised. However, it is better if the stamp is in fact a low-level currency in a merit system that rewards students' overall achievement in the school. The stamp should link in with certificates and letters of congratulation to the students' parents. It is far better for all the teachers in the school if they work as a unified team. Therefore, if all teachers use a low level reward like a smiley face in similar situations it will encourage pupils to respond in the same positive uniform way. Even if this is not the culture of the school, and everyone is doing his or her own thing in terms of punishment and rewards, you must create a system with which you can survive in your own classroom, but ensure that it is not so time consuming that it becomes a rod for your own back.

The smiley face is a very flexible and practical reward. It can be used with high frequency without seriously impeding the flow of the lesson – being very quick to administer. A whole class that has behaved well can have their books stamped in two minutes. Individuals can be rewarded in a matter of seconds. It is much quicker than the teacher initialling or putting a signature on something. This makes it invaluable in difficult classrooms where multiple rewards are needed regularly, every lesson.

Letters of praise and certificates

The quick recognition from the ink stamp is ideal for dealing with short-term needs or one particular lesson. But to give them more effect on pupil motivation, they need to link cumulatively to certificates or letters which go to parents. Writing these is clearly more time-consuming than stamping but it is time better spent than writing copious letters whining and complaining about the misdemeanours of certain students in your lessons. The parents who get them will have usually had many from other teachers throughout that child's school career. They hardly ever contact you to make an appointment, which your letter suggests they should. They probably shout at or, in certain cases, hit the pupil in question for being bothered by the letter but this kind of action is hardly constructive in changing negative behaviour, as the inner-city school experience shows repeatedly. Some parents are at their wits end with their own children and simply ignore your letter, and others will believe that their own son or daughter is being singled out by the teacher, simply because their children tell them so. If they contact the school at all to speak to you, it is to voice their complaint.

This is the reality of the kind of parental contribution that many of your worst lesson disrupters have behind them. It takes a long time to write or type a letter and address the envelope. If you are going to invest this time, the good letter, certificate or letter of improvement will get a more useful and positive response from parents who are already so jaded with bad news. For them it will be a breath of fresh air to get a positive communication from the school.

Positive reward chart

It is well worth keeping a chart in your classroom of those who have received a certain amount of smiley faces or who are getting lots of merits certificates, whatever the currency, in your subject. It is time-consuming to do but will keep pupils fully involved in the system. They will actively enjoy looking to see how they are doing.

A whole class reward

Likewise, it is also worth trying to build a whole class reward into your positive reward system. For example, reminding the whole group periodically through the lesson whether their mark out of ten for good concentration and good behaviour is going up or down. The aim should always be to create a situation where the barometer is rising, so that all members of the class are swept along in the upward momentum of the lesson. Each class member could receive a smiley face if a 10 out of 10 was achieved, or maybe the class will get some kind of star on their chart for this kind of excellent lesson.

The advantage of a whole class reward is that it can help you get a whole group to concentrate and maybe work in complete silence – a rare and hard to obtain quality situation in a difficult school. When there is a whole class reward to be had, peer group pressure will often stop the most malignant individuals from spoiling the atmosphere by talking or mucking around. Yet the whole class reward should never be the only thing you are prepared to give out in a lesson.

Remember, the bottom line is always: 'However hard a lesson, you are always looking to reward those individuals who are doing the right thing.' A whole class recognition is just an extra, on top of that basic system.

Phoning home

This is usually more effective than a letter as a real two-way communication can take place from which some positive targets for the pupil can be set in mutual agreement with their parents. But it is often difficult to find people's parents at home during the working day, and in schools with very poor intakes, telephones are forever being cut off or are never installed. It is often hard to concentrate on taking notes of your phone call for the pupil's personal file. The letter has the advantage of being written and easy to add to the pupil's record as evidence. It is also quicker to pen a short note than talk to a parent on the phone for twenty minutes. If you decide to write a missive, you can do it on the spot, whereas if, as a busy teacher, you have to constantly re-dial a parent's number, you'll probably forget to do anything about it eventually! Teaching is a very pressurised and rushed job and a whole new set of emergencies and priorities will come from teaching next day's difficult classes. The smiley face is the quickest way to reward, the letter is the second quickest and surest and the phone call is brilliant, but only if you get through first time and can do it quickly.

It is always best to praise and reward rather than admonish and punish. The pupils who verbally abused you must be dealt with in some way and we shall talk about practical punishments later. But the pupils who were verbally abusive last lesson will most effectively change if you can reward something they have done right in the next lesson, thereby breaking the cycle of confrontation and negativity. The 'good' letter of praise that goes home, reporting an improvement in a pupil after a bad patch, will work more for you in the long term than a bad letter informing the pupil's Mum that you were told to 'f*** off'.

Calling parents

This is the best way of dealing with parents and is most likely to effect a positive change in any pupil you teach. However, it is very time consuming; an interview could take half an hour of your very precious time. Also, in a difficult school you will probably request to see many parents in any given week.

If you see a parent, make sure that you keep a written record of what was said in the pupil's personal file and give a copy of the record to the year head and tutor.

Seeing a parent will make a lot of difference to a pupil who has just been antagonising you and should know better. For the very difficult pupils, it will probably do no more than keep that person at bay and make them think much more seriously about crossing you in the future. The 'keeping at bay' result is very important if you are to survive and succeed with the rest of the class. Your interview with a parent will be most fruitful if you stress anything positive you can say about their son or daughter.

Many parents in difficult schools often threaten and bludgeon their own kids in front of you if you make a complaint, and you can tell they are going to take x or y home for a good 'pasting'. This is not the sort of support you want from them. Always try to suggest practical things they could do to help their son or daughter and the school. Other parents will be aggressive, will take their own child's viewpoint and will accuse you of picking on their son or daughter. In these situations, try to placate them in order to avoid a counter-productive argument in front of the pupil, and, for the file, simply write down a front of the pupil, and, for the file, simply write down a list of the items discussed and the way they were received. Parents who take this line are not going to be any help to you in your battle to survive. It's best to leave them to senior colleagues and serious incidents.

In many schools contacting parents and asking to see them would be frowned upon unless you first spoke to a middle manager such as a year head. In the difficult school there is seldom time for such niceties and your senior colleagues are only too pleased to see you trying to sort out your own problems in this manner. They'll have plenty of other parents to see for other teachers about serious disciplinary matters. You are saving them time and hassle. They will only put a stop to your independent actions if your letters, phone calls and interviews lead to parental complaints and lots of follow-up work for them.

Chapter 2

Sanctions and rewards

SANCTIONS

Difficult schools are inundated with punishments and sanctions. And yet for all the endless punishing, there are always pupils who need punishing. The number of permanent and temporary exclusions is usually high, but it is only the tip of the iceberg if you consider all the terrible acts of verbal abuse, bullying, fighting and lesson interruptions that occur every day. Clearly, punishment has not worked and is not the way to improve many difficult schools.

I would suggest that you must think long and hard about the type and amount of punishments you impose. For every detention, bad letter home, etc., there should be at least five rewards on average.

Having said that, you must also have some sanctions, but they should be designed to be as effective and as practically workable for you as possible. It is one of the biggest myths of the school system that, by constant and consistent punishment, children are motivated into learning better. The more difficult the behaviour of the pupils in the school, the more futile is the system of constant punishments.

What kind of sanctions work?
(For you and the pupils)

1 Sanctions that don't waste too much of your time. Just something symbolic that makes the point about who is in charge.

2 Ones that are carried out as close as possible to the misdemeanour. Most disruptive students have short-term memories. Sanctions will need to be usable with very regular frequency, not just once a week.

3 Ones that you actually carry out easily. If you try to hold back members of a very difficult group, they could push past you or run out of the room. Ask a lot of students to come back after school and many will not turn up. Do it on the spot and you can get it over and done with. Don't make sanctions that leave you with a lot of chasing.

4 Ones that you can get regular help with, if a class is difficult. It is always good to let pupils see that teachers support each other in matters of discipline and work as a team.

5 Ones that are fair. Always try to identify key trouble-makers and sanction them, rather than hold the whole class back as a sanction.

Some tips on detentions

What I am about to say about detaining pupils is going to be controversial. There are many teachers who would disagree strongly with me. They will argue that long detentions are a vital deterrent and will help you impose your will on a difficult group, if applied consistently. I disagree. Your main weapon against a difficult class will always be rewards, your ability to interest them in what you are teaching and setting work at the correct level.

Having said this, short detentions are a good way of getting the last word with a pupil or pupils who have continually disrupted your lesson and refused to involve themselves in your rewards culture that day. Detentions are most effective if they are short and available as an option as frequently as possible. Therefore, it is easier to deal with your end of school session classes than with groups you only see at the beginning of the afternoon or morning. In difficult schools the most troublesome pupils will not turn up for an end-of-day detention that you set in the morning, so try to enlist the support of their form tutor or their last teacher and ask those colleagues to retain the offenders until you arrive. The smaller the number of pupils and the quicker you get there, the more workable will such a solution be. Heads of year and heads of department will soon get bored with you if you constantly refer long lists of students who have failed to turn up at one of your detentions. You must learn how to use their help sparingly, only when you most need it.

They are under too much pressure themselves to provide you with round the clock support and servicing.

Remember that the big negative with detentions, whatever type you use, is that they are another forum for a lot of negative confrontation with pupils.

'Why are you keeping me back? I didn't do anything wrong. Why me and not X? I'm not staying for your detention. I've got to pick up my little sister.' You will often get this hurled at you in a difficult class. In a truly horrendous group that has had a very difficult and unstable lesson with you, people will try to run or push past you in order to avoid staying.

If you try to use the worthy strategy of letting good pupils go and only keeping the bad ones, they will try to sneak out at the same time. Really crazy ones will climb out of windows (especially if you are on the ground floor) to avoid staying back. You are very likely to get into verbal and physical confrontation and the situation could easily escalate out of control.

The conclusion with detentions has to be that they are only possible when you do have reasonable control over most of the class, so that the people you are punishing are clearly seen to be in the wrong and are less likely to become aggressive about it. But in a 'barnyard' lesson, the lines of right and wrong are lost in the general mayhem. Try not to use immediate after-the-lesson detentions then.

You are probably better advised to seek help from within the school and contact parents.

I don't suggest that you punish yourself by setting long detentions in a difficult school for pupils who have not done their homework. Again this is a controversial opinion as many teachers in difficult schools will waste hours of their time getting little Johnny or Stacey to write 10 lines of 'near rubbish' in an enforced session. Later, I shall return to the subject of homework and other strategies for getting more out of the pupils.

Other sanctions

As an ordinary classroom teacher there are precious few options available to you. The letters home, phone calls and the seeing of parents have already been mentioned as time consuming but useful. It has also been mentioned that you should try to make your contact with the parents positive and constructive, and not merely 'complaining and carping'.

Sending pupils out of the room

This is even more controversial among teachers than the use of detentions. The split occurs between the senior managers (who don't like to see disruptive pupils in the corridor as they may often wander off and cause chaos somewhere else) and the classroom teachers (who are at their wits end, trying to get a lesson momentum going and dealing with one or more students who are hell bent on destroying the lesson).

In a difficult school, there are pupils like this in every class. They can spoil the whole lesson because they won't stop running around the room, shouting and screaming or bullying others. There would seem to be nothing else you can do with them, other than at least temporarily get them out of the room.

My suggestion is that you try to compromise with the nervousness and reluctance of your senior managers to do this.

In certain situations a pupil must go out!

1 If you regularly have a problem with a certain individual or a group, try to get an agreement from a teacher in a nearby classroom that he or she will take the group in for the rest of the lesson.

2 If somebody is behaving intolerably and blocking you from teaching a whole class, put them out! But tell them that it is a 'two minute time out' and you want them back in the room when they have decided to be sensible. Don't leave a pupil outside for more than five minutes if you can possibly avoid it, even if they don't make the decision to be good. The time outside will probably have calmed them down.

3 Don't send more than one pupil at a time outside your class, unless it is absolutely unavoidable. This is a recipe for corridor chaos and you'll upset your fellow teachers as they will probably get disrupted as well.

4 If your school has a referral unit – that is to say, 'sin bin' – for just these kinds of situation, then don't be ashamed to use it. It is not a sign of weakness to use all the school support systems. Just a few words of practical advice: you will usually have to fill in a form to get someone into such a unit for the lesson, and fiddling

about with that is likely to further destroy the momentum of the lesson. The more pupils you try to send there, the more forms you will need to fill, thus lengthening the time your eye is 'off the ball' in the lesson itself.

5 Increasingly Schools have department or faculty rotas. Teachers in the same subject areas, take it in turns to absorb one or two difficult pupils from each other's classes. Experienced teachers can often manage one more in a class. Even inexperienced teachers can manage an occasionally challenging pupil imported in their lesson, if they have an especially reasonable class at the time. Getting a belligerent pupil out of their class is like removing a over sized fish from its accustomed bowl. In a different room, they have to re-acclimatize and for a while they will be disorientated, if they find themselves in a top set Year 7 when they are in Year 10 or vice versa. Using a rota can often be a much better support system than a 'sin bin' or 'time out' room. It will often cause less confrontation with the pupil to have a colleague take them into the class next door rather than go to a room in another part of the building, associated with being punished. But like any system you can send one, maybe two, from you most difficult class but not seven!

6 Remember that, in a difficult school, the pupil you try to send out may refuse to go. You will then have created yet another difficult confrontation situation and may need external help from a more senior colleague. Getting that help will further disrupt the lesson as you will have to write a note and persuade someone in the class to take it (which is not always easy).

It is always better to use 'sending out' as a threat, rather than an actuality. If you give the pupils a sensible choice – either you stop doing that or you'll go out – many will opt for the first. There are some pupils in a difficult school who are dying to be kicked out of the room so that they can meet up with other internal truants and do other things. You must remember also that some pupils will be even more disruptive outside your room than in it. They bang your door or make faces through the glass at members of the group. They may even shout comments back into the room.

All of these things are considerations before you put a pupil out. Having said this, I do believe that in very difficult classes there is often no other option if you are to gain lesson momentum!

Giving an effective telling off

One of the essential skills you need to learn in a difficult school is how to tell a pupil off effectively. The opportunities to do this without being ignored or answered back can be hard to engineer. You raise your standing when you can take the moral high ground with a pupil and get the last word. You reinforce your reputation as a pushover if you tell people off and they treat you in a publically derisive way. On the other hand, you begin to establish yourself with the whole class when you get the upper hand in admonishing a pupil for his or her wrong doing.

Here is a simple list of factors that you should take into account before you give a telling off. As always, there must be a balance between gaining dominance in an interchange and avoiding a confrontation which you end up losing.

1 Try and pick off the individual, who is most challenging of your authority. If possible, take them away from the peer audience they will be wanting to show off to. If you have to take them on in a lesson, take them to the side and out of ear shot or outside the classroom for thirty

seconds. Even better if you can save the most difficult individual tellings off until after a difficult lesson.

2 Stay aware of your own body language. The more you feel panic, frustation and inadequacy, the more your body will tense and spoil the effect of the telling off you think you are doing. Pupils read your body language for the real message and often ignore the actual words coming out of your mouth.

3 If you are dealing with a crowd control situation in a corridor, make your requests to pupils and then give them time and space to follow your instructions. If you stand over them, they may fear too much loss of face in front of their peers, to follow your commands.

4 Don't panic. Stand your ground and repeat instructions calmly and purposefully.

5 A little bit of humour and light heartedness with pupils, that leads to coaxing rather then commanding is often highly effective. It also keeps your body from tensing up.

6 If pupils refuse to follow your instructions or flare up rudely, it's best not to get into a big confrontation about it there and then. Follow them up later. If you follow up, you never really lose a confrontation or your dignity. You give yourself a second chance to get the last word.

7 But once you decide to follow up, you must remember to do it. Forgetting to follow up would be disastrous in establishing your authority in the school.

8 The most effective tellings off are when you can gain the moral, intellectual and emotional highground from the pupils. If you follow up, you can prepare what you will say and where you will say it. You can visit the pupil in a lesson later in the day or week and ask them to come out. You can request that a Head of Year or a form tutor is with you, to back up your authority. Pupils are always impressed when they see their teachers working as a team.

REWARDS

A school system of non-rewards

This is the opposite of a merit point, gold star and smiley face. Some schools will have a slip of paper for you to fill out on a pupil who disrupts your lessons. This has some practical use as a relatively low-level sanction:

1 It is usually quick to fill in. You can do it after a lesson and students cannot confront you about it in the same dangerous way as if you are trying to keep them for a detention against their will.
2 If it is a school-wide system, the teachers will be presenting a similar set of responses to bad incidents by filling in the forms. It creates a uniformity which is always useful when handling school-wide behaviour difficulties.
3 If the non-rewards are collated properly, they can lead to a whole school punishment or interview with parents etc. The children who have general bad behaviour at school are thus identified.

A non-reward is a useful sanction but it takes a lot of time and effort to reinforce an essentially negative system and negative culture. It would be far better to organise a system of rewards that is used in the entire school before worrying about organising the reverse.

Human nature in difficult schools will also tend to make teachers use negative non-rewards more liberally than positive rewards in difficult classrooms.

When a sanction becomes a reward

The best way to use the majority of sanctions is to twist them into rewards. I am talking about the 'forgiveness' factor. For example, that five-minute detention that was imposed for bad behaviour can be taken off if the pupil modifies his or her behaviour and finishes the rest of the lesson well. The student who is continually talking and gets a non-merit could work that off by working silently.

CONCLUSION TO SANCTIONS AND REWARDS

To survive and succeed in a difficult school you must change the way you think. Reward, reward and reward. The more difficult the class, the more rewards.

When you feel yourself about to explode and give a series of non-rewards, detentions, etc., think positive and try to find some individuals to do the opposite for.

Remember prevention is always more effective than cure in a tough school. Reward is an effective prevention; punishment is not an effective cure.

Remember: behaviour management is the key in a difficult school. You cannot even start to teach unless you've got it somewhere near right. You will have to spend a significant amount of time every day catching up with your reward charts, seeing parents, detaining pupils, etc. This is unavoidable and is the penalty for working in a difficult school. The more systematic you are, the less serious confrontational crises you'll have. These 'one offs' can be just as time consuming and more stressful.

CHECKLIST ON SANCTIONS AND REWARDS

Sanctions

1 You should use them as sparingly as possible.
2 Ignore and override your impulse to punish rather than reward in a difficult classroom situation.
3 Ignore your colleagues who talk about how hours of detentions break down resistance from difficult individuals.

It is one of the biggest misconceptions of behaviour management. Think about how some individuals are always in detention and it has failed to change them one jot.

4 Sanctions are a negative response to situations where there is already much negative behaviour.

5 Use sanctions only as a simple counterpoise to your rewards system.

6 They should be little and often if they are detentions (5 minutes will be long enough).

7 Remember that detentions can lead to confrontation and may be unenforceable, especially after a riotous lesson where the difference between right and wrong got blurred.

8 Don't use detention as a regular punishment for not doing homework.

9 Don't detain a whole class, keep targeted troublemakers back – the fewer the better.

10 Try to avoid sending pupils out of your lessons.

11 In difficult schools, this is sometimes unavoidable and in those situations try to just send one student out for a short two-minute cooling-off period.

12 Unless it is an absolute emergency, don't send out more than one.

13 Remember the very act of trying to send someone out might create an insoluble confrontation that will damage the lesson more than the behaviour that the pupil was exhibiting.

14 Remember: the removal of a sanction for improved effort and behaviour is almost like a reward. This is the best way to use most of your sanctions.

Rewards

1 You cannot use them too often.

2 Rewards such as a smiley face stamp are brilliant for quick, flexible, low-level use.

3 Low-level reward currency should build into a system of formal recognition with certificates and 'good' letters home.

4 Ideally, what you do should tie into a whole school system, as it will then work better for everyone.

5 If it doesn't, build up your own personal system and stick to it. Pupils will still respond positively within your classroom walls.

6 Have a wall chart to show individual and whole class progress week to week.

7 Accept that you will add an extra half an hour minimum to your day keeping charts and writing certificates and 'good' letters home.

Chapter 3

Routines and strategies

ROUTINES AT THE BEGINNING OF LESSONS

All children need routines. Pupils in difficult schools need them even more urgently because their behaviour is so extreme that they need to know that there are reassuring parameters to contain them. You can make the school routines your classroom routines as far as that suits you, but in a difficult school many of those routines will be only figments of the imagination written on behaviour policy documents that are often unenforceable. So leave anything that you cannot insist on as a routine in your classroom. Chewing gum in lessons and dropping litter may be best ignored in a horrendous class but followed up in a class that is more pliable. The worst thing you can do with a difficult lesson is to try to enforce so many routines that you never get the lesson momentum in place.

Therefore, stick to very basic routines that you can enforce. They are vital because they are symbols of your control in the classroom. By obtaining what you demand in terms of certain simple procedures you'll create a situation in which you can do some teaching. If you fail to carry out your own basic routines, your lesson is unlikely to stabilise. Remember that you should have certain teacher routines in the same way that the pupils have their routines.

Teacher routines

- Try standing at the door to greet pupils individually as they come in. (Say something friendly, even if it is only 'Hello', followed by a name.)
- If you are still packing away from the previous lesson as your next class comes in (sometimes unavoidable), then try at least to have a quick word to key individuals about what they must try to do to have a good lesson. Point them towards a particular seat.
- Find reliable students who are always on time and get them to give out lesson materials and exercise books while you are sitting the class down and getting coats off.

Pupil routines

- Pupils should come in and sit down in seats, two to a desk and facing the teacher. They must not expect to turn their chairs away from you or sit four or five around a small desk. They must not start moving the furniture to spoil your seating plan.
- Pupils should take their coats off and put them by their sides or on the back of chairs.
- Pupils should bring basic equipment to lessons such as a pen or pencil to write with. If they do not, they can expect a small punishment from you.
- Pupils expected time of arrival is within 5 minutes of the lesson change-over sounding.
- Pupils will build up small sanctions if they get out of their seat without permission and start walking around the room.
- Pupils who do come in, sit down and wait sensibly to start the lesson should be rewarded as an encouragement to keep on being positive role models to the others.

You must fight for these basic routines each and every lesson as some members of the class will always 'try it on'. In difficult schools you must win on the 'general expectation' of what the routines will be. This means that the majority of pupils will obey your routines with minimal fuss. A prime feature of a difficult school is that a minority of very disturbed and poorly motivated pupils will often try to defy your routines every lesson before they settle. So the battle is never completely won and you must expect to ask some individuals to take off their coat many times in one lesson before they comply. On another occasion they may test you by arriving very late or by making a big fuss about working because they don't have a pen or pencil. You must know what your ground rules are and stick to them. There will always be some struggle to enforce them but your struggle would be much greater if you did not have them at all.

If you are having to struggle with certain difficult individuals about taking off their coats.

1 Remind them that you were very pleased with them last lesson because they did it.
2 Repeat your instruction that they must take off their coat very calmly. If the situation in the room permits it, go up and say it to them in a personal one-to-one way as this will usually work much better than shouting publicly across the room.
3 Give them time to comply with your instruction before you repeat it.
4 If you are making no progress and a confrontation seems to be inevitable, it may be best to disengage and try again later for the sake of the momentum of the lesson for the other students.
5 If you decide to 'stand up' there and then to the challenge, try to give the offending pupil a choice and on a one-to-one basis, say: 'You either take your coat off or get a five-minute detention'.

6 Any punishment you threaten must be carried out if the pupils refuse to take the choice you have set up for them.

7 It is best if that punishment can be left until later so that it is not something that has to be argued about at that moment, causing more confrontation and interruption to lesson momentum.

8 If you find yourself in a major 'no-win' situation in which the pupil is determined to flout one of your ground rules, then delay the confrontation until after the lesson or to any time that suits you. As long as you do this calmly and confidently you will avoid losing face in front of the class and will not find yourself with a situation in which everyone is putting coats back on again. Ultimately it is better to have a good stable lesson in which two pupils keep their coats on, than a terrible lesson which never gets started because you are in a screaming match with the same two pupils about their coats.

9 If the lesson goes well and the coats stay on, don't forget to follow it up. If pupils see that they can regularly break your few simple ground rules and get away with it, more will do it over more things.

10 However irritated you begin to feel, try to stay thoughtful and calm. Most pupils will have obeyed you and most pupils want to have a good lesson. It is your overall job to ensure that you can get this to happen for them and you most certainly will not if you start 'foaming at the mouth' over a couple of coats that won't come off. We often get angry as teachers because the behaviour of some of the pupils makes us feel insecure in front of the others. We feel silly asking for something from young people who are ignoring us while other youngsters are watching. It is, however, important to keep things in proportion. The youngsters who watch our authority being flouted will see

many other teachers struggling with the same difficult pupils and many may well sympathise with our predicament, even if they say nothing.

Obviously in classrooms where the level of friction is lower and the level of motivation higher, your list of routine expectations can rise and include:

- Your expectation that the class will not chew gum or drop litter. If you see pupils doing it, you will immediately insist that they pick it up.
- Your right to move pupils away from friendship groups to sit on their own.
- Your expectation that the class will come into the room and work in silence.
- Your expectation that they will spend parts of a lesson working in silence.

Push for these when the possibility of establishing them will not lead to endless aggression and confrontation.

So this should be a constant expectation of how routine lessons can go in a good class and a occasional routine if you sense you are having a good lesson with a bad class. Be an opportunist: if you are having a unusually good day, make the most of it and push for more. One of your central challenges for self-improvement with a troublesome group is to turn the occasional routines into regular ones as you tighten your grip on them over a period to time.

ROUTINES AT THE END OF LESSONS

The end of a lesson is also a five-minute slot of critical importance, second only to the first ten minutes of a lesson. The main challenge is that pupils stop working in anticipation of the lesson ending and start wandering around the room or trying to leave early. (Many try to pack up with fifteen minutes still to go.) If you have had an effective lesson you can feel more relaxed about the way it is likely to end, as the forward momentum you have established will make your job easier when you come to tie up the learning experience. If you have had a very patchy lesson which has been a constant battle, then the last five minutes will be even more important and the difficulty of getting them 'right' that much harder.

Again, there should be basic routines, but you should not have too many and should stick religiously to the ones you have so that pupils are reassured by knowing exactly what is expected of them.

1 Get the pupils to sit on their chairs, so that there isn't movement around the room. If people are wandering, disturbances can break out.
2 Have a routine for collecting exercise books, resources, etc. In some classes it may be easier to ask the pupils to put them into piles in front of you as they go out. In others, find a couple of sensible pupils who can collect things for you and give them long enough to do it.

   While they are doing this, you can concentrate on calling people by name and persuading them back into their seats.
3 Try to have a central focus to the last few minutes. Ask a question that carries a reward. Encourage someone to come up and run through the main points of the lesson orally. Ask what was the most interesting thing they think they learned that day. Try to do a short quiz or a series of word squares on the board that encompass the key learning points of the lesson. It is important that your lesson ends with a constructive feel rather than fizzles out like a damp squib. Leave the pupils with a strong sense that something energetic and useful has just happened to them and that the lesson ended with an 'event' of some kind. (See more details in a later Chapter.)

4 Keep them working until the last few minutes. Don't give in to the temptation of starting to pack up too early. It is better to have a slight rush to pack while maintaining the lesson momentum than a flaccid atmosphere in which people are getting bored and waiting for the bell to ring.

On the other hand, don't leave too much to the last moment as your lesson will inevitably end with a feeling of rush or confusion and will probably end late, causing you more problems as your next class riots in the corridor or starts barging into your room.

TEACHING STRATEGIES TO BEGIN LESSONS

Teaching strategies are not quite the same as classroom routines, although many of your teaching strategies will become 'routines'. The key to success is to regularly use certain teaching strategies so that the pupils are reassured by the familiarity of your approach and expectations. But, as usual in teaching, there must be a delicate balance between routine that bores through its monotonous regularity and variety that keeps pupils stimulated and on their toes.

The best compromise in a very difficult class in a rough school is to have a repertoire of routine teaching strategies to start lessons – ones that you have used many times and found to be successful. As far as possible the routines should contrast each other. By varying the 'set starts' the pupils will not notice that they are indeed a set of 'routines'.

The first rule of teaching strategies is to dismiss those that are bound to destroy your chance of starting a lesson well:

1 Don't embark on a complex piece of group work that involved lots of alteration to the way that pupils have sat down.

2 Don't try a complex piece of group work that involves you giving out lots of written and verbal instructions that pupils will have to wait and listen to for a long time.

3 Don't try to insist on a long period of time when you and/or a series of pupils read aloud.

4 Don't turn you back on the class for a long period of time and try to write work on the board.

5 Don't expect to speak about anything without interruption for 10 minutes. They will not listen.

6 Don't take a register and insist that pupils listen in silence.

7 Don't try to talk to pupils who have their seats turned away from you.

8 Don't try to talk or shout over the noise of pupils who are still talking to each other.

9 In some classes at certain times of day, don't talk to them at all as a whole class. Certainly not as a teaching strategy at the beginning of a lesson.

Some good beginnings of lesson 'teaching strategies'

1 No big group work exercises. Some simple pair work. Jazz it up by giving out marker pens and large pieces of sugar paper. Get the pairs to brainstorm an idea as a bubble diagram. Give them a time limit. The pupils will let off some of that excess steam they seem so often to bring to their next lesson by talking about a solution. The exercise works well if there are lots of open-ended answers that allow for maximum positive participation and rewards for those who are prepared to report back to the teacher, who can put lots of ideas on the board. The good thing about this strategy is that it involves a lot of people positively in a forward propelling momentum. The minority that will not settle can be dealt with

individually as the majority get on with a relatively noisy open-ended task.

2 Have something simple written on your board, such as a paragraph of writing or a simple 'close' exercise for pupils to get on with as soon as they come in. Settle each troublesome member of the group down to that task, and only when most people are busy writing away, calmed with simple work, do you, the teacher, try to start the lesson. This strategy gives the better pupils something relatively useful to do which does not need any explanation, while you get on with settling all the class into their seats.

3 A quiz, with its simple competitive edge, is a better way of galvanising the attention of an unruly class than the more traditional 'this is what we are going to do today' type of beginning.

4 Any situation in which questions can be answered and rewards given to those that answer is a good way of getting attention. (This is particulary effective when a smiley face stamp is used.)

5 Paired reading rather than whole class reading is a good way of starting a difficult lesson as it is less confrontational and can be done in a relatively noisy room. It also allows you, the teacher, to 'jostle' individual pupils into action by explaining what they have to do.

6 Tell a vivid story. Do some simple role play, calling for volunteers from the class to help you. This is much easier to set up on the spot than group work. You can get a good pupil illustrator to come up to the board and draw a picture of what you are saying.

Entertainment is the key to success in a difficult class. If you have something interesting to say which you can relate to the pupils' daily life experiences, you have a much better chance of getting their attention. (See later chapters on ways of using ideas that entertain and tap into

pupil experience.) Underpinning any teaching strategy for your first ten minutes must be the frequent use of rewards. They will help galvanise the attention and move the lesson into a forward momentum whatever the strategy you have used. They will help soak up and reduce the aggression and negativity that some of the pupils are giving out as they try to prolong not settling down for the lesson for as long as they can. If rewards are administered with the balance of low-level sanctions they will be even more effective. As soon as a pupil who has chalked up a sanction begins to behave well, then it can be removed. The most telling sanctions, as discussed earlier, are those that can be worked off when positive behaviours begin.

BODY LANGUAGE AND WAYS OF SPEAKING TO AVOID CONFRONTATION

All teachers have different personalities and it would be stupid and naive to write this section, offering advice that ignores this.

Some teachers get quick and effective results for themselves in difficult classes in tough schools by fighting fire with fire. They use aggressive body language, point fingers in pupils' faces. They shout down opposition and bulldoze their way into getting the last word. They frighten, shock, intimidate or bully dissenting pupils into silence.

I have seen this and you will also see this work effectively. The teacher in question gets a result without using any rewards or sanctions. The surge of energy or ego from that individual is sufficient to quell most difficulties. For these teachers, this approach works! Therefore it is the right one! As a result of it, they are able to create an atmosphere in which they can teach effectively.

It is important to recognise that this works only for a small minority and cannot be copied with success. Too often other teachers try to copy the 'blockbuster' approach with stunning failure. They do not have the personality to out-confront confrontation and they make things much worse for themselves.

I believe that the great majority of teachers need to forget the macho approach to discipline adopted so effectively by some men and women in difficult schools. The method of bullish confrontation and barrack room discipline are out of place in our profession. Ultimately the learning situation cannot thrive on coercion or aggression to achieve its ends. Learning is a contract based on co-operation and not on force. So most teachers should try to stay calm and relaxed and lower their voices when faced with aggressive and negative pupil behaviour. They must try to overcome a natural adult reaction to feel embarrassed and 'shown up' when other pupils and teachers see their authority countermanded publicly. When this happens, many teachers seek to defend themselves by shouting and stoking confrontation with pupils. They need to redefine the situation away from confrontation. Very few battles with difficult pupils can be won by protracted shouting or long detentions. Some students get endless detentions from many of their teachers but it doesn't change their behaviour.

A key to success in a difficult school is to look for role models that can be copied effectively because they are using sensible non-confrontational tactics with the pupils.

Effective body language and ways of speaking

1 Try to keep your body frame relaxed. Every time you feel yourself tensing with frustration or irritation, breathe deeply and rock on your heels.
2 Try to talk politely to pupils whatever the aggression in their voices.
3 Try to talk privately to pupils whenever possible, rather than having to shout across a classroom of eager listeners. This may mean going to a pupil's desk and

bending or kneeling down to speak with that person. Remember: the bigger the audience, the more likely that the pupils will feel the need to play to the gallery.

4 Look pupils in the eye when you speak to them. Asking somebody to do something and then looking away is unlikely to convey your personal confidence or resolution to them. If you fail to look at them in the first place when you give the instruction, then you can expect to be ignored.

5 Keep on thinking about points 1 to 4 no matter how browbeaten you are beginning to feel. Body language and ways of speaking need your constant personal attention throughout the lesson if you are to survive. In very difficult lessons it can be as important as all your teaching strategies and materials put together!

THE ENTERTAINMENT FACTOR

Relating learning to what the pupils already know

In difficult classes this is more than just a cunning teaching strategy – this is an absolute must! The National Curriculum has taken a lot of freedom and flexibility from the difficult schools in the name of standardisation and quality control for all secondary schools. If you had gone to your average difficult secondary school in the mid-1980s you would have found a very different curriculum. It would have been much more flexible to the needs and interests of the students. For example, in History many of the Key Stage Three courses would have included topics that were much less of a British History heritage trail than they are now. There would have been a greater variety of social and world history topics. English would have had a wider variety of texts in use than is possible now. At Key Stage Four there was much more scope for schools to draw up their own courses, which could then be accredited for public examination. But the tests at 11, 14 and the new GCSE syllabus, with their greater emphasis on exams than course work, and league tables for schools, have removed a lot of variation and inventiveness from the taught curriculum in favour of standardisation.

Put bluntly, this has made it harder for teachers in difficult inner city schools to make their lessons relevant and interesting to their pupils. They have to stick to what everyone else in the country is doing when that classroom norm is often very different to the classroom conditions of difficult schools. So the challenge is to make the more academic National Curriculum interesting to the pupils.

In terms of History, the subject that I teach, it is very difficult to teach the structure of the nineteenth-century Conservative and Liberal Parties to 14 year olds who do not have a great intellectual interest in this subject. Yet this is the Year 9 National Curriculum.

The best way to 'survive' in inner city classes when you are being asked to teach a diet which is going to make your survival even more difficult is to bend the rules as far as possible and seek to identify parts of the course which are 'user friendly' to your pupils – that is to say, bits which are entertaining and even draw easily from their personal experience.

Let's take National Curriculum History as an example. A study of the Industrial Revolution up to 1900 in Year 9 should look at the policies and personalities of the Victorian Conservative Party. To try to teach these as they were, would be a recipe for complete disaster. But if some of the basic ideas are taken from Victorian times and applied to the students' knowledge of how the country is run today, the experience will come alive. The trick of making History entertaining in difficult classes is to highlight and spend more time on those topics that will hold the attention of the pupils. So the way that children of their own age were treated as workers in mines or mills will get much more attention than looking at figures which compare steel and coal production for Britain and Germany. All the time the teacher must look for what is practical from the past and apply it to the pupils' daily experiences. So get a pupil to crawl under a chair and point out to the class that this was the height of the tunnel in a mine. Time a pupil running across the classroom to pick up a paper ball from the floor and then explain to the class that they would have had to go faster to avoid getting trapped under a carpet press. Ask students with long and short hair to come to the front of the class then ask the class which one would be safer working in a nineteenth- century factory. Find a good picture of child labour and get the pupils to look at it carefully – a good picture is worth ten times the value of a piece of writing in getting pupil involvement in a difficult class.

Given that two of the greatest problems working in a difficult school are getting and holding the attention of pupils, you must be constantly looking for ways of providing entertainment. You have got to make your intellectual points effectively and quickly in that kind of visual, practical and colourful framework. The pupils would not otherwise concentrate to read the same information, dryly out of a text. For many, reading is something they find boring and difficult. They are far more likely to comply with your wish to do some after you have given them a taste for the topic in a more immediate and direct way. For teachers in difficult restless classes, the need to convey facts quickly and colourfully is overwhelming.

Entertainment checklist

1 The National Curriculum is there to frustrate you. In most subjects it narrows your choice of subject content.
2 Because of this, you need to be more thoughtful when planning your teaching approaches to what has often a more 'boring' content.

3 Wherever you can, miss out something, especially if it would have bored your class into even more extreme restlessness than usual.

4 Concentrate on those parts of the curriculum that you can make more entertaining.

5 Use pictures and short dramatic role play whenever possible.

6 Try to decide your main point before the lesson begins. See if you can find a 'contemporary' and practical way to illustrate it, drawing on the pupils' own experiences.

7 Be an opportunist. If you find that through entertainment you have grabbed their attention, then press on to the less colourful and more complex ideas that you were afraid they would be too bored and restless to listen to.

PREPARING YOUR LESSON MATERIAL

'Differentiation' in lesson materials was one of the buzz words of the nineties classrooms in secondary schools but it will always be a vital teaching skill. To survive and succeed in difficult classrooms you must learn to dip in and out of differentiation as it suits you.

The most important way you can differentiate in a difficult and restless class is to plan you lesson material to involve as many pupils as possible quickly and effectively. So it is best to make it an easy open-ended task to get people started. If creating something truly open ended presents problems, then simply make it easy so that few pupils are left scratching their heads, wondering what to do.

Differentiation by task for different levels of ability is a favourite with Ofsted Inspectors but it can cause major problems in an already difficult and fractious classroom. Students soon pick up on who is being given a simple piece of work because they are 'thick' and will often refuse to take what is being offered. The high level of achievers will often argue for the simpler work as they don't feel like concentrating on anything too taxing that day. The giving out of different work to different pupils can lead to dangerous resentments and confrontations on top of the ones that the teacher already has in starting a lesson. It creates a lot of extra work in terms of preparation and duplication.

Differentiation by open-ended assignment presents other practical difficulties to the harassed teacher in a difficult class. It is very hard to think of questions that are genuinely accessible to a wide range of abilities. So the danger is that some people will finish the task very quickly and superficially while others take much longer. This could throw your lesson organisation into chaos.

It is probably most practical to differentiate by stepped outcome. For example giving out materials that start with easy questions or closure exercises but become more difficult, leading to questions that require long detailed answers.

This type of stepped task is less discriminatory and labelling than giving different pieces of work to the various pupils. It also provides the teacher with the opportunity of setting plenty of work for everybody.

In a tough classroom it is vital to keep the pupils busy. The resourceful teacher will always have just one more exercise up his or her sleeve. Nothing will dislodge the successful momentum of a difficult class more than pupils running out of 'things to do, which they can do'.

Teaching materials checklist

1 Differentiation of work materials is very time consuming, but it is a necessity, especially when pupils have reading ages well below the level of most standard textbooks. In a difficult school, a majority will have this problem in almost every class.

2 Differentiation should involve as many pupils as quickly as possible. Keep opening exercises simple so everyone can try them.

3 Differentiation by task can cause problems with some pupils who feel they are being labelled as 'thick'. If you are going to give out different work to different pupils you will create confrontation, unless you can think of a very clever way of selling it to the class.

4 Differentiation by stepped tasks is more effective. It has the advantage of being 'inclusive'. Everyone is given the same thing to do and some just get further than others. In terms of teacher organisation, it is usually easier to handle.

5 Whatever the differentiation rationale for your lesson materials, always have plenty of work for the pupils to do. If they run out, it's a recipe for trouble.

ON THE SPOT DIFFERENTIATION FOR WEAK READERS

In every class you teach in difficult schools, there will be a large number of pupils with low reading ages. The average textbook has a reading age of twelve plus and many disaffected pupils have never got beyond a reading age of a nine year old. These pupils soon become bored and frustrated with the standard diet of educational publishers. So you need to find ways of simplifying difficult texts quickly and effectively.

Here are some vital ways of opening up a difficult text quickly:

• Write the key words for lesson on the board. Explain them.
• If you are going to use a text, explain what it is going to be about in advance in simple language. What can the reader expect? This will help and re-assure the poor readers.

- Are there any pictures in the texts you are using? If so, can you ask for any open ended questions about them. Pictures are very good way of getting everybody involved.
- When you want the class to do some writing. Explain very clearly what you want them to do. Give the same clear and simple instructions again to pupils with literacy difficulties. Individually, if you get the chance. Get them to repeat those instructions to you, using their own words.
- Write an example of what you would like to see the pupils' writing. Put it on the board as a model the whole class can copy.
- Sit the poor reader next to a good one. Allow some paired reading in the lesson. Make it explicit to the good reader that you want them to help their neighbour.
- Make up a simple written exercises, using the key points of the lesson and put them on the board, as the lesson draws to an end. Do it off the top of your head. Get *all* pupils to complete it in the last five minutes. It will be especially helpful in reinforcing the main points of the lesson for weak literacy pupils.

Interactive whiteboards

Increasingly teachers have interactive whiteboards which they can type these little exercises straight onto. Unlike boards that use chalk or dry marker pens, exercises can be stored and put back on the screen for another lesson. You can enlarge the font size if you need to. Providing the IT is working, this is a great innovation and beats wobbly handwriting any day!

Quick 'on the spot' materials

The secret to much successful teaching is the opposite of what the experts tell you to do, that is to say planning all your materials before you go into the class room. To survive and succeed, lesson after lesson, you need to plan the broad sweep of your lesson in advance but be able to think on your feet and write some exercises for the pupils 'on the spot' – that is to say, off the top of your head.

Highlighting

Highlighting can make a good 'on the spot' exercise. Provided you've given out something photocopied that can be written on, pupils can be asked to highlight the text. If you have coloured pens to give them for the different things they are underlining, even better.

You can pick a short bits of writing, not the whole page and ask them to look for some very simple things. Highlighting is a useful quick exercise. Some good things to do with it include:

- Underline all the sentences, which include the key word you have just written on the board.
- Find out the names of all the characters and highlight them.
- Find all the words that describe the way that character x feels.

Cloze and True/False exercises

There are many kinds of exercises you can prepare but few are as easy and simple as Cloze and True/False. The teacher can create these on the spot.

In a typical cloze exercise, you write a few lines summarising the main messages of a longer piece of writing. The pupils have to fill in the blanks. The easiest way for them to do this is if you give them a short list of missing words for them to tick off. The secret of success is to keep this list short and select a very brief part of the overall reading to base this exercise on.

Another winner is True/False. You test their knowledge of the text by writing a series of statements. Some are blatantly true and others are false. The more obvious the statements, the easier the exercise. The pupils write them down and tick the correct one and mark the false ones with a cross.

The beauty of both these types of exercise is they encourage pupils to do quite a lot of writing but much of the information they are using has already been scaffolded by you. All they are doing is adding to it. Simple activities like this act a low entry level exercise that keep some pupils learning purposefully, while the more literate pupils can engage in more complex manipulation of text, appropriate to their competency level.

Working with pupils with English as their second language

Many inner city urban schools are the first port of call for refugees, just arrived in the country. You need to prepare yourself to cater for the needs of a refugee who had just arrived in the country, escaping from the Taliban regime in Afghanistan. Or a pupil who had seen his family killed in political repression in Kurdistan. If you start teaching in most urban areas in Britain, these and similar scenarios are a real possibility. Some inner city boroughs have a huge proportion of pupils who have a mother tongue, other than English.

The quicker you find out everything you can about these English as a second language (ESL) speakers in your class, the better. They will have come to England in very different circumstances for very varying reasons. Some already have high levels of literacy in their own language and they are likely to make rapid progress in English, their second language. However others will have backgrounds where there is very little reading or writing experience. The way you handle these pupils' will be very different.

As that teacher, you should work on the basic principle that most strategies you can adopt to help ESL pupils will have the double benefit of being good techniques for teaching all of your pupils better. Start by looking at the reading materials you are using in advance. Do they include language and cultural concepts that the recently arrived pupils will find hard to understand? Technically, how are the sentences and the paragraphs constructed? ESL pupils often find it hard to deal with linking words such as 'therefore' and 'however'. They also find sentences which begin with pronouns which connect back to an earlier noun, very hard to follow. If you find the texts you are using have a lot of the challenges such as the ones I have described, then you could use some simple strategies to make those reading materials more accessible. A recent arrival could be sat next to a more established pupil of the same cultural background so that they could converse in their mother tongue to make sense of the work. If that pupil has been through similar emotional experiences to the newcomer, then they might be able to offer even more benefit in the settling in process.

Working with ESL pupils can be deceptive. Within weeks or months they may be communicating fluently in everyday English but they are far from fluent in more complex forms of oral and written English – especially the formal and abstract language use that underpins the higher order literacy skills of the National Curriculum. As a classroom teacher you will have an important role in creating a language rich environment to help them make progress in these vital skills. First, by helping them develop their oracy. This can be done by setting up a lot discussion about a topic in small groups before writing takes place. Oral work that involves the rehearsal of key words and concepts, with plenty of reinforcement and repetition is a vital activity.

You should also model types of writing in different genres, so that they get used to the written conventions of their new language. Too many teachers assume that they will pick up these skills by instinct, but it's unlikely to be that easy. A science teacher will need to show ESL pupils how to write up experiments. In particular how to write in the passive voice so that 'I put the test tube in the bunsen burner' becomes 'the test tube was placed over the bunsen burner.' A history teacher needs to show pupils how to write discussion and analysis rather than stories.

All of these strategies make good teaching sense to second language pupils. But they will also help open up the curriculum to special needs pupils and help the vast majority of pupils who need explicit teaching of literacy skills. The strategies that help ESL pupils are completely in step with the intentions of the National Literacy Strategy for all pupils.

Chapter 4

Marking work

As with differentiated lesson material, the importance of marking has become central to the critique of good and bad teaching in the minds of Inspectors and school managers. It is, in my opinion, a much over-rated and ridiculously time-consuming occupation when taken to the extremes that many teachers spend on it. In difficult schools, it does have a useful purpose to fulfil in enhancing the motivation of the pupils but only if a balance is struck between marking and all the other pressing priorities of a busy school day. It should never take priority over effective lesson planning and following up a simple rewards and sanctions policy in the classroom.

MARKING: THE DO'S

1 Do it regularly. Regularity (quantity) is more important overall than depth (quality), especially in difficult classes.
2 Be realistic. You could have between 6 and 10 different sets of 30 pupils' work to look at each week. So marking each set once a fortnight is good practice.

3 Mark quickly. Even English teachers need to learn this skill. You cannot read every word that they write. Be selective. This could mean giving all you time to one specific exercise and ignoring everything else done over the two-week period.

4 Pinpoint a couple of grammatical error and spelling mistakes. The better the motivation of the student, the more point there is to this kind of marking.

5 You should be able to write at least a sentence-length comment on each book; either that or two phrases. Use the pupil's name in your short comment as a personalised remark is more apt to be read.

6 Your comment should use simple language and be easily readable. Without this, writing anything is just a waste of ink and time.

7 Your comment should praise anything of merit and keep the target for improvement to a few simple words.

8 If there is a departmental grading system, use it. Pupils will be able to get a relative level for themselves by seeing at a glance whether their grade is going up or down during the two-week periods.

9 If you can insist on some simple spelling corrections in class time as a result of marking, then do. It's a good way of getting pupils to actually take your marking a bit more seriously.

MARKING: THE DON'TS

1 Don't spend more than one hour marking a set of books, unless it is a very special marking assignment. If you do, you will lose too much of your precious time to an activity which is not your most important priority in a difficult school.

2 Don't write long critical comments; they will probably not get read properly by the pupils. You are not writing comments for Inspectors or heads of departments who

might be auditing your books at some time in the future.

3 Don't keep on writing the same critical comment if it is not getting any pupil response. Simply refer them back to the comment you made before or say something new about their work instead.

The key purpose of marking in a difficult school is to keep up a regular dialogue of encouragement and praise to the pupils who are working hard. It is a way of rewarding them with a bit of warmth and appreciation in a short written comment. Marking that is constantly negative and in laborious teacher scrawl is simply going to turn pupils off.

However, the one time that a troublesome pupil does do a brilliant piece of classwork or homework, marking can be used as a way of reinforcing this effort through a praiseworthy comment.

In general terms, marking enables you to build up an impression of what the individuals in your class can do and respond well to. In difficult schools marking is best used as a tool to reinforce your attempt at controlling difficult classes through the positive reinforcement of written praise.

FORMAL ASSESSMENT AND TESTING

I would suggest that regular formal assessment of pupils in difficult schools is also a good way of maintaining their motivation. It is also a better way for the teacher to work out what they actually know and need to learn next, than the fortnightly marking of exercise books or folders.

At a classroom level, the teacher who is able to dramatise the importance of his or her own assessment tests is likely to obtain a more purposeful working atmosphere. Inexplicably, pupils who are often restless and poorly motivated in what they consider to be an ordinary lesson, will work like the, 'clappers' in a formal test situation. The more clearly the teacher has been able to explain the purpose of the test in advance – that is to say, the learning objectives they are looking for – the more eagerly the class will settle to its task.

Clearly pupils of all abilities and motivations respond to the factor of competition. Whether it is right to subject them to continuous testing in which their achievements are compared unfavourably with those at better schools is debatable. It is also doubtful if there is any point in setting them national tests at 11, 14 and 16, which many simply cannot do because they cannot read them properly.

But teacher assessment set at a level at which pupils can show what they can do will give the teachers who advertise its importance more control in their lessons. Assessments at regular intervals also helps focus the pupils on the learning they are supposed to be doing, which makes them a useful tool in the teacher's range of options.

Chapter 5

Homework

A NATION-WIDE AGENDA OF 'BLAME'

Homework is one of the most controversial issues in modern secondary school education. Its importance is continuously declaimed by politicians, Inspectors, school managers, parents and ex-pupils. The most-common criticism that parents will make of schools or teachers is they are not setting enough homework. The first cry of most teachers is that they set homework but many pupils don't do it and their parents do nothing about it. The teachers blame the parents who blame the school. The politicians blame the Inspectors who blame the schools.

The obsession with homework seems to stem from public school civil servants and Members of Parliament who remember their own days at public and grammar schools, where they got lots and lots of it.

HOMEWORK IN THE CONTEXT OF A DIFFICULT SCHOOL

Difficult schools are made up of students who come from disadvantaged socio-economic backgrounds; they are schools to which few middle-class people send their children. There is no tradition of homework in the communities from which such schools draw their catchments, so when the teachers ask for homework to be done, they are going against the cultural grain. The pupils have found ways of not doing their homework and it is easy to play parents and teachers off against each other. 'It wasn't set' often means 'I decided not to write it down in my diary'. Many parents accept what the child tells them when they see a blank page or the words 'none' as a homework entry. They are not regularly looking at their children's school work and don't pursue the matter. They themselves, despite what they claim, probably did not do much homework either. Teachers who are continuously using up valuable time thinking up homework tasks and then using valuable duplication money producing them, eventually get demoralised when only a handful of homework tasks are returned out of a whole class. They then try to punish pupils who haven't done their homework by giving them detention. They start to contact the parents to tell them that homework is missing. As a one-off measure this will often get the child to do it, but on the next homework assignment that same student will draw a blank again.

Chasing up homework is one of the most time-wasting activities of any teacher in a difficult school. Ultimately a very large majority of pupils are simply not going to do it, whatever strategy is tried. They are not motivated to do it. Their parents often pay lip service to supporting the teacher but at heart they don't really care. So the teacher is backing a loser and it is vital to accept that reality.

Save your energy for finding strategies to get more homework out of the pupils who often or always make the effort to do it.

Why setting and checking homework is important

Despite the fact that so many pupils in a tough working-class school will habitually fail to produce homework, setting and checking it is a valuable asset in your classroom survival kit.

Adopting routines around setting and getting home-work will enhance your status as a teacher in difficult classrooms.

Homework checklist: the positives

1 A substantial minority of any of your classes are troublesome in lessons and never do homework, but you owe the enthusiastic and hardworking pupils the chance to do extra work at home.
2 When someone does homework regularly, they add a huge amount of weight and depth to the written work that they are doing for you.
3 Homework gives the motivated pupils a chance to fol-low up the interest and enthusiasm they showed during the lesson. Teaching is all about tapping into these kinds of energy. In a difficult school it is very hard for you to give these individuals much time in a lesson because of other problems in the room. But homework gives you a chance to build up a learning dialogue with some pupils when you mark their books.
4 By setting and checking homework you establish another important tool of control. The pupils know that the school expects them to do homework, even if they hardly ever bother. They will respect you for struggling to uphold the letter of the law. If they don't do their homework, they know you have 'got one on them' for the whole of the lesson. This is a reason for behaving and working well for you.
5 A homework check at the beginning of the lesson gives you an immediate opportunity to reward those who have done what you want.

Homework: the negatives

1 Checking homework 'one to one' with the pupils takes time and in a rowdy class this could lead to

serious behaviour problems as people get bored of waiting.

2 While the minority of well-motivated students take a lot of trouble over homework, many others do the bare minimum just to get you off their back. Five thoughtless and hastily scribbled lines is hardly worth all the fuss of checking. It will probably have an educational value of nil.

3 Whatever strategy you use, many students will not write homework down, using such excuses as they haven't got their diary with them or there isn't room in it to write all your instructions. They will often leave your homework sheets on the desk absentmindedly or deliberately as they rush out at the end of the lesson. You are wasting your time and precious resources trying to get these pupils to do homework. Their parents will often have the cheek to ask that you personally write their homework down for them. Don't to it. You cannot do it for one and not for the other ten or so pupils who have exactly the same memory lapse. Writing it yourself is still no guarantee that the pupils will do it. If you give in to this kind of pressure, you might as well go the one small step further and do their homework as well.

STRATEGIES FOR GETTING 'MORE' HOMEWORK IN DIFFICULT SCHOOLS

As usual you will get more homework if you reward rather than sanction. People who insist that incomplete homework is done that day in a detention are simply making a rod for their own backs. Pupils made to do homework under duress seldom become regular high-quality homeworkers as a result of the experience. So some useful strategies are:

1 Give a reward stamp (smiley face) to all those who can show you they have done the homework when you check it.

2 Use the school system, if there is one, for recording homework completion. If there isn't, then make up one of your own.

3 Accept that a 100 per cent return rate is unrealistic and that you will be doing well if, in some classes, you raise the return from four to seven students regularly and that, in more motivated groups, a rise from 40 per cent to 65 per cent will be excellent.

4 Send the occasional homework missing slip to parents of marginal students who should know better and might respond constructively to this kind of surveillance. Contact parents who respond positively to information and don't waste your time on the ones who never do anything or try to bounce the problem back onto you.

   Remember: you simply do not have the time to enjoy a weekly dialogue with individual parents about the completion of their son's or daughter's homework. It is something you can only monitor intensively for very short periods of time. In all homework monitoring you should take no more than 40 minutes of your time outside the classroom every week. If you spend longer, you are cutting precious time away from far more important priorities.

5 Get students who have done good homework to read it out in lessons. Give them lots of praise.

6 Display good homework on the wall of the classroom. It always pleases the students to get such public recognition for their work.

7 Try to keep a homework completion column on your rewards chart, so that pupils can see how they are doing. This is another good way of rewarding the homework do-ers and creating a bit of healthy competition.

8 Every so often bring out pieces of homework that you tried to set before but pupils didn't do, and encourage them to improve their own completion rates by doing

them late. Late homework is much better than no homework at all.

9 In a truly terrible group where you are struggling all lesson to keep them in their seats, don't worry if you sometimes forget to set homework. There are other more pressing priorities.

10 In a class with an appalling homework return, try the strategy of only setting homework as an honour and privilege for a few pupils. This could turn the concept of homework on its head and engender some competition. Anything is worth a try.

Overall, try to encourage good practice by rewarding good example rather than by constantly punishing bad or incompetent practice – that is to say, those who never do their homework.

Chapter 6

Support teachers

THE INVOLVEMENT OF SUPPORT TEACHERS

Getting support teachers to work positively with you in your lessons is also vital to your 'survival' and 'success' in a difficult school. It is likely that some of your classes will attract an extra teacher who is charged with the responsibility of supporting one or two pupils on statements or looking after other students who are at an early stage of learning English. You may also receive some support from a special needs teachers if your group has many pupils with very low reading ages. Increasingly learning support assistants are replacing teachers in this role. They are cheaper to employ and schools get more adults into the classroom for their money.

Whatever you get in terms of additional support, it will never be enough. The majority of the pupils that you teach would respond very positively to one-to-one attention or being taught in a very small group. Their social and intellectual disadvantages cannot be addressed in a normal classroom but the resource implications of this are so immense that the politicians prefer to tell you that the real problem is your bad whole class teaching.

So when there are two teachers in the room, make the most of it. You must squeeze as much as you can out of that second professional, in the nicest possible sense.

Making the most of your support staff

There is much benefit to be had from a second adult in your classroom – teacher or teaching assistant. If you want to maximise the benefits, then you have to work out the strengths and weaknesses of the characters that are joining you in your classroom and make the most of the qualities on offer.

The vast majority of your support staff are full of energy, commitment and ideas and will support you one hundred per cent. Very experienced and well trained assistants can team teach with you, prepare the kind of differentiated lesson material described in Chapter 3 and can even go round and mark exercise books.

The most wonderful thing about having an effective support assistant is that they provide you with psychological security. You feel happier in even the most troublesome and restless groups because you have another sane adult to measure your difficult experiences by. It removes the feeling of personal frustration that can be very isolating for a teacher on their own and reminds you that its not your fault that some pupils behave as badly as they do.

But learning support assistants require a lot of guidance about how they should work. You will need to tell them what you want them to do in your lessons and in some cases, model the good practice that you are hoping to see. In my experience, classroom teachers are often too passive about the way they work with teaching assistants.

Strategies to maximise the role of your learning support staff

- Meet up informally for five minutes between lessons, to plan for the next one.
- Introduce the teaching assistant to the class properly, so everybody knows that he/she is there for an important

purpose to help pupils in that class. It's best that any special relationship to weak readers isn't stated, too overtly, to avoid a negative spotlight on their difficulties.

- Try to put the pupils who need extra support in a little group around the assistant.
- Encourage the assistant to work in different ways with the pupils. Sometimes taking them out of class, other times working one to one or in small groups in the class. Encourage the teaching assistant to be flexible about letting you do this. If you have a good working relationship with them, this is much easier.
- Show them how to simplify work on the spot, during the lesson and make up little exercises for the pupils they are working with.
- Model the process of going around the room to annotate/mark work for literacy skills. Two people marking books gets through more books and gives individual pupils, more professional time.
- Try and get your classroom assistant to help all the pupils from time to time, whatever their literacy needs. It's good for them to be like a bee pollinating all the flowers, not just the ones that are not doing so well. It will raise their status as an adult with knowledge and expertise amongst all the pupils. Even more importantly, it will take the spotlight off pupils with weak literacy. They are already likely to be ashamed and embarrassed about being singled out for help a lot of the time.
- Some whole class teachers can draw and write as they speak to a class. Many find more than one activity at a time difficult. If you are busy explaining something, you should encourage your assistant to write key words and phrases on the board. He or she could do a flow diagram to represent these ideas. (This kind of impromptu arrangement for working should be exploited, whenever possible.)

Chapter 7

The importance of equipment and resources

THE CONTEXT IN DIFFICULT SCHOOLS

Lots of pupils in difficult schools don't bring pens, pencils and basic equipment to their lessons. They then use this lack of equipment as a reason to disrupt others and do no work. If they are allowed to take their regular classwork exercise book or folder home to complete the work, they will lose it or be too disorganised to bring it back.

The more pupils without exercise books and pens at the beginning of a lesson, the more chance that your lesson momentum will be blown to pieces. You must be prepared with a whole range of strategies to minimise this kind of pupil disruption.

SOME PRACTICAL STRATEGIES

1　In general, keep your pupils' exercise books in your classroom. Don't let them take them home.
2　When you set homework, give them something else to take home. There are a number of systems you could adopt.

- A homework folder.
- A homework exercise book.

- Sheets of lined paper that can be taken home and then attached to a classwork exercise book or file.

3 The loss of a classwork book is a disaster to young people whose motivation and momentum are already patchy. Any written work that you have got them to do successfully in lessons over a long period of time, and all your encouraging written comments in the book, will be lost at one stroke. They may well be too lazy or disorganised to bring their books back to a lesson once taken away, but they are still likely to say that it was you who lost their books! They will refuse to work on paper, saying that there is no point. They will exhibit irritation and despondency at not having their exercise books to write in. The more you try to convince them that it is they who have not brought back their book to the lesson, the more confrontational the situation will become and the more disruptive to your lesson momentum. You can avoid most of this by keeping the treasured classwork books yourself. It is much better to risk the homework not being done than to lose all the work!

4 What do they do with their books? They are left at home, left in other teachers' classrooms, left on the bench in the playground and dropped down the side of a cupboard in a classroom. Often you will find them on the floor in the classroom as an eager student has rushed out at the end of class. Behind this is a profound symbol of many pupils' lack of real pride and interest in the work they do for you. A substantial minority try to avoid carrying a bag to school, so they obviously have a problem with carrying books around all day. Others reserve the space for carrying illegal school footwear such as their trainers, which they change into given any opportunity. I have found that pupils who actually finish their exercise books cannot be bothered to take them home and I am forced to store

them or simply throw them away when my pile gets too high. For many the work that they do for you in a lesson is just the 'here and now', they will often work hard to please you but they are not interested in looking at any of it again, ever! This creates an exercise book equivalent of writing on a slate and then rubbing it out at the end of each lesson. Keeping their books carefully for them is a way of getting these pupils to recognise that their books are important.

5 Remember that, for most pupils, the time they spend working in their lessons is much greater than the time they spend on homework. This is the stark reality that you must learn to live with.

6 Giving out extra folders, homework exercise books, sheets or whatever you decide, is a costly and time-consuming exercise that could create new organisational problems for you in terms of marking, storage and classroom management. But these are far outweighed by the grief you'll get by having lesson momentum disrupted by the minority of students who will turn up to a lesson without their classwork exercise book.

7 On the quiet, without most pupils knowing, you can allow your most reliable pupils to take their exercise books home. You will soon get to know who they are. It can be done as a kind of secret privilege for all their co-operation and hard work.

8 Always have spare pens and pencils in a handy container which you keep hold of. Never put anything like this down in a difficult classroom as somebody will nick it.

9 If you hand out material, keep a note of who it has gone to and make a super-human effort to remember to get it back at the end of the lesson, otherwise you will lose tons of equipment every week. It is best to avoid lending equipment easily though, because

people begin to rely on the fact that they can turn up empty-handed and borrow it.

I recommend a policy of encouraging them to borrow pens and pencils from each other. I explain to them that, as a last resort, I'll lend them something to write with, but if they come to me there will also be a small penalty to pay. In this way I minimise the amount of equipment I lend out. One routine is not necessarily better than another. However, once you have decided on it then you must stick to it ultra consistently. I am always forgetting to get equipment back in the flurry of an end of a lesson, so restricting the amount I give out is, for me, a better routine.

10 If you have a difficult group, don't add to your problems by getting them to share textbooks or worksheets. It will make it very difficult for you to move or isolate a troublemaker if people are sharing material.

11 Try very hard not to get angry when a pupil to whom you have just lent a pen or pencil says it cannot be used because it doesn't write properly, will make his or her handwriting untidy or is the wrong colour ink, etc. This is simply another tactic to disrupt the lesson, 'wind you up' and do no work. It is a ploy that will be used frequently.

Chapter 8

Gaining lesson momentum

I have suggested a whole range of practical strategies that you can try to gain control and forward momentum in your lessons with difficult classes in hard schools. But there are some underlying paradoxes to the situations in which you work that are irreconcilable.

RIGOUR VERSUS NON-CONFRONTATION

To survive and succeed you must press forward, you must demand that the pupils concentrate and progress. Yet this very act requires that your body stiffens and tenses. In a restless classroom with many half-hearted pupils you live in constant expectation that you will be disobeyed. This adds naturally to the tenseness in your muscles and the tightness of your voice. I believe that the processes of 'demanding', 'pushing' and 'squeezing more out of' all lead to this stiffer body state. I cannot imagine that any teacher pressing for more in a classroom does not feel a certain amount of body tension creeping in. You would only stay relaxed in a learning situation where you were 100 per cent confident of the motivation and compliance of your students.

Yet in the aggressive classrooms of difficult schools there is the equally strong counter-pull of needing relaxed body language and relaxed mind to continually diffuse or side-step situations of confrontation. Therefore the two expectations placed on teachers are utterly contradictory. The classroom professional is expected to switch from one mode to the other repeatedly during a lesson. Only years of experience, familiarity and confidence with a particular school's pupils could help you even begin to do that. In many ways the dilemma of tension versus relaxation is impossible to solve properly. It has to be a clumsy 'fudge'.

THE BALANCE BETWEEN 'INSISTING' AND 'IGNORING'

Knowing when to insist that an individual takes a coat off or moves to a different seat is also something on which it is difficult to give precise advice. Sometimes to survive and succeed you must insist, even if that means to confront and risk yet another interruption to lesson momentum. At other times it is the wrong thing to do, and ignoring the problem, however severe, would be the right thing.

The pressure from on high and outside is always to demand high standards through 'rigour' and to insist on all the small things being right, on the basis that this is how to win with a difficult class. But in reality this is not always the best policy and is just not enforceable. The teacher of a wild class is being asked to insist on or ignore issues a hundred times a day. The frequency of the challenge to their right to teach is exhausting. It is rather like a tennis player facing a very fast service game after game, being asked to return the ball every time so that it beats the server. The level of concentration, energy and body stamina required to win every time is impossible!

You will only 'survive' and 'succeed' if you find a balance between conquering problems and compromising with them. Like a successful tennis player you can still win a match if you win key points against a heavy serve and break once in a set – to win every point against sustained attack isn't feasible.

THE VOLATILITY OF THE PUPILS

Finally it is worth remembering that difficult classes tend to be tremendously volatile. They will behave terribly one lesson and then the next time you see them they will cooperate like little angels. Sometimes you can link their behaviour patterns to the time of day or to the teacher they have just left, but there is an x-factor which cannot be explained logically. As a classroom teacher in a difficult school you have to expect these kinds of ups and downs and not be too disappointed by a bad lesson after a couple of reasonable ones. Just remember that each of these really difficult groups has as many as ten or twelve troublesome characters, capable of having a funny turn at the drop of a hat. It only takes one serious quarrel between two of them to seriously disturb the atmosphere in the whole group and rock the lesson momentum. Sometimes you are going to lose the battle and then the most important thing is to lose gracefully and avoid having a complete screaming fit.

OVERALL STRATEGIES FOR GAINING LESSON MOMENTUM

1 Positive rewards – lots of them. (Create your own system based on your own strengths and weaknesses.) You can never use them too often!
2 Some carefully thought out sanctions. (Quick, short and easy to administer frequently.)
3 Give the pupils the chance to choose between right and wrong whenever possible. This should also include forgiveness.

4 Routines at the beginning and end of the lessons, that you insist on consistently.

5 A repertoire of teaching routines in the first critical ten minutes of the lesson that help 'minimise' negative confrontation and help you get the students to listen and read.

6 Body language and ways of speaking to students that avoid confrontation, whatever the provocation.

7 The importance of clear ideas which are colourful and entertaining to capture and hold the channel of communication, if you can get it. In particular, relate learning materials to experiences from the pupils' everyday lives. Nothing will work if you can't catch their interest.

8 Plan your lesson materials to involve as many pupils as possible quickly and effectively. Better to make it easy to get people started.

9 Stay calm, whatever the provocation. Breathe deeply and rock on your heels as you feel your temper rising. Getting angry is neither in your nor the students' best interest.

10 Regular marking of work and lots of praise.

11 Stressing the importance of assessment to the pupils, so that they are very clear what skills you want them to learn.

12 Generating a little healthy competition with regular small tests and quizzes. The pupils respond well to it.

13 Enlisting help from classroom support teachers and/or other colleagues.

14 Have spare pencils, pens, etc. Always have enough worksheets or textbooks. Sharing is a recipe for disaster and reduces your options to move pupils around the room.

15 Break up friendship groups, but be careful about how you do it.

16 Try to raise the momentum of your lessons by making a big deal of setting homework and checking them. It will help your classroom control.

The don'ts

1 Don't set yourself up for a series of momentum destroying confrontations.
2 Don't get so angry that you sap all your energy 'ranting' and 'screaming'.
3 Don't panic, even when the situation is not looking hopeful. If you hold your nerve the situation could still turn in your favour.
4 Don't insist on calling a register at the beginning of the lesson. This is a recipe for early confrontation.
5 Don't line classes up outside your door as this is also the recipe for early and serious confrontation.
6 Don't pile on a series of threats and sanctions, especially ones that punish the whole class and not individuals.
7 Don't be inconsistent with your own rules.
8 Don't give work that is too difficult or needs too much explaining in airspace that you cannot get. This is a recipe for disorder and chaos.
9 Don't expect to give a long speech. Ten minutes of uninterrupted speech would be a miracle; less in the afternoon and then not necessarily at the very beginning of the lesson.
10 Don't waste too much time preparing copious written lesson plans.
11 Don't turn to write on the board in a very volatile class.

Part II

Your wider role as a school teacher

Chapter 9

Life outside your own lessons

THE AIM OF THESE SECTIONS

This part of the book will look at your survival in your role as tutor, general dogsbody doing lunch, break duties or cover and the challenges that being in these roles as a figure of authority will present you in a very tough school. It will also examine the biggest conspiracy of all – the gap between what you are told you should be doing to be a solid successful professional and what you must actually do to survive. We shall look at how to manage the crisis of time shortage and high stress levels and whom to go to for help and support.

DEALING WITH SCHOOL MANAGEMENT

In a big secondary school, 'management' means middle and senior management. They cannot be treated in the same way as they fulfil very different roles in a school. To survive and succeed in the classroom in difficult schools, you must understand who to go to for help and the frequency with which that help can be called upon. You must learn when to say 'yes' and 'no' to managers. It is sensible to make the general rule that it is best to stay friendly and co-operative with both levels of management and you will do that if you say 'yes' as often as possible and combine that with not making too many demands on them.

KEY POINTS TO CONSIDER ON 'MIDDLE MANAGERS'

They are first and foremost classroom teachers like yourself as well as heads of year or heads of department. They are managers, but they get very little extra time to manage and their remuneration for the extra responsibility is only a small part of their overall salary. You are 100 per cent a classroom teacher and they are 90 per cent teachers. Don't expect them to be able to work miracles for you. They need your help and support as much as you need theirs. You will soon comprehend that their relationship with senior management and with each other is often full of tension and conflict in a difficult school.

They will also be struggling with 'mad' classes, maybe less or more than you. So they will not have all the answers to your problems. You must share and suffer together. They will also be struggling with their roles as a middle manager, which combines the administration of the department (ordering books, equipment, doing examination entries and preparing communal lesson materials) with the curriculum side that writes and revises schemes of work. There is an increasing expectation from senior managers that they take a more proactive role in improving the teaching, learning and exam results of their subject teachers like you. This increasingly means sampling teachers' lessons, feeding back and setting targets formally with them. They will often be sorely stretched by these increasing demands on their performance.

Use them sparingly

1   Accept the basic premise on which teaching in tough schools takes place. You must consume as much of your

own smoke as you can. Don't try to funnel it all off on your direct line manager.

2 Balance this by not being too brave. You must admit to difficulties if you are having them. Asking for help, however experienced you are, is not a sign of weakness but strength. It is responsible to get support sparingly but irresponsible if everything is passed on.

3 Middle managers vary. Some are very supportive and others are not. Some will use your requests for help as a way of showing off their own power with the pupils and some will support you with practical 'low key' help, advice and back-up. The former are useless, the latter are life-savers. You need to learn who to go to and who is a waste of time. Job definitions of who is supposed to do what are useless for the ordinary teacher in a tough school. You go to the person who will help you in your classroom. It is vital to find out the strengths and weaknesses of your line managers and make the most of the former, bypassing the latter whenever possible. Lingering on your line manager's weaknesses is a recipe for a bad relationship.

   Realistically you will often need help and it is best to go to a person whom you know will support you, irrespective of what the school handbook says.

4 Relationships can be especially difficult in situations where two people line-manage each other for some aspect of work – for example, a head of department who is a tutor and a head of year who teaches English.

   If you are in that situation and don't get on, there could be great stress and tension. Compromise is the best way to keep the relationship going reasonably. In a difficult school people are often feeling so stressed that they find this very difficult.

5 Don't allow a middle manager to bully you whatever his or her status. If you feel this is happening, then you must warn that person that you will go to a senior manager as an arbiter. Such assertive behaviour will make you feel

better in the long run. It is draining to have to endure the unreasonable demands and pressures of bad daily relationships. Obviously it is better to sort out your differences with that person yourself rather than move on to a strategy that they may find threatening.

How can your middle managers help you?

As a general rule, the pupils understand and respond when they clearly see that teachers are working together as a team. They have worked out that a teacher in isolation is much more vulnerable to attack. The very act of working in partnership doubles the number of adults that can be brought to bear in a difficult situation. It cuts the ratio of adults to pupils and is therefore a good idea.

Strategies a middle manager could use

1 To come into a room and help you settle the class down at the beginning of the lesson. This is most effective if it is you who holds centre stage, with them hovering in support on the edges.
2 To take out one or two very difficult pupils at the beginning of the lesson and talk to them individually about their behaviour, while you settle the class down.
3 To give you the offer of sending a couple of disruptive pupils to them (either in their lesson or departmental office) if you feel it is necessary during the lesson.
4 To offer an after-school or lunchtime detention in which you can put pupils as a stepped sanction if they have failed to turn up or did not stay back for yours.
5 To offer a departmental rewards system for you to use, which they preside over. This could involve the middle manager coming into your class and praising those who have done well. Again pupils will respond positively

to more teachers knowing about their success in the same way as they react to teachers backing up each other in times of difficulty.

6 To give you practical tips based on experience, either formally through meetings or informally in your daily contact with them.

7 To be present when you see pupils who are causing regular problems, and to assist you when talking to their parents.

8 Some of this help and support would come from a head of year and some from a head of department. The more difficult the school, the more blurred the who, what and when actually becomes.

9 In theory it is usually head of year for incidents that occur outside lessons or are cumulative across all subjects. Heads of department are supposed to line manage problems within lessons. In practice, the most difficult schools produce their own adaptation of this principle. This is likely to be a compromise of the above systems that revolve round the strengths and weaknesses of the actual individuals concerned.

10 Help and support is a two-way process in education. There may be many occasions when you could offer to do any of the same things the other way round for a hard-pressed middle manager. There are likely to be a whole host of situations in which he or she will be glad of your team support in a difficult school.

Obviously you have to gauge when offering this support is appropriate and when it would be 'frowned' upon as a threat to that other person's status and self-image.

However, this should never occur if it is offered in the right spirit.

11 You will get a much more sympathetic ear from all your middle managers if they see you battling away conscientiously to solve your own problems. They will

respect you for using your own rewards and sanctions to consume your own smoke. They will be relieved if you try to learn strategies that avoid constant shouting matches and confrontation with the students, which take long periods of time for a third party to 'unlock'.

12   You will get into their good books if you mark regularly, write reports on time and volunteer to prepare new materials for schemes of work. Heads of year will be pleased if you keep your register up to date and are prepared to contact parents and act as first port of call to teachers who are dealing with your tutor group.

Conclusions

You will get more useful help from middle managers if you are seen to help yourself and others by trying hard to fulfil your role in the school. In difficult schools, it means accepting that a lot of time and nervous energy must be used on 'working it out for yourself' with very difficult classes. There is no way round this.

The supportive help that you can get starts to make more sense when you have already won the basic respect of most of the pupils and are achieving a positive learning experience in some sort of rough and ready way.

Beyond a certain level of 'chaos' friction and confrontation, support from middle managers can dampen down the fires that rage in your classroom but cannot put them out on your behalf. Realistically the middle manager will become as frustrated with supporting you in a 'no-win' situation as you are for being in it. Classes which fall into this level of disequilibrium claim many detentions, letters home and exclusions, but despite all that time and energy, none of the retrogressive actions seems to make any difference.

The class has become like some kind of multi-headed serpent out of a Greek myth. Lop off one head and another grows in its place. The more that are got rid of, the more exclusions are needed. After all there are always 'nutters', excluded from other schools in the locality, who are just waiting to come into your under-subscribed year group.

A good middle manager

A good middle manager will be a good strategist and team leader. He or she will know how best to 'pull strings' in the school to help the department and year team, of which you will be a member. That person's help can extend well beyond involvement in the practical strategies that I have already described to make your daily classroom life easier. He or she will plan ahead for improvement and change. For example, the schemes of work for a new syllabus will not be left until you start teaching it, and new materials will be written ahead of time, using all the skills of the members of a department as a team effort.

A good middle manager will be sensitive to your needs to develop your skills as a teacher and a manager. He or she may delegate specific work or departmental responsibility to you to give you a chance to learn. This kind of effective manager will get you to do more work without you thinking that it is an imposition and that you are 'being dumped on'. You will be part and parcel of a team and feel that you are pulling together, even if things are difficult. If that same line manager gains your trust and respect you will let that person watch you teach and give you constructive advice on how to improve. Quite simply, having a supportive 'proactive' hardworking middle manager on your side is one of the best ways to survive and succeed in difficult schools and rough classes.

SENIOR MANAGERS

Background

Assistant heads, deputy heads and heads do have a different experience of the school day to middle managers and ordinary classroom teachers. In secondary schools they have varying teaching commitments, but they are lower in all cases than the other groups.

Heads seldom teach more than a couple of hours each day; deputy heads have between 25 and 45 per cent and assistant heads between 40 and 60 per cent loadings. This means that the school day feels very different for this level of staff. However, if they are performing their roles effectively, they will have plenty to keep them busy.

Management at senior level

School management at senior level is becoming forever more complex and involves a large variety of 'whole school' initiatives – some new, some one off and many cyclical with each year. It has its own strains and pressures which the ordinary classroom teachers do not understand, due to lack of experience of it. However, there are important differences in the daily experience of senior management and the rest. The more difficult the school, the more chance that communications between the two of them can be poor as both groups are feeling seriously stressed.

Senior staff inevitably become preoccupied with their own managerial initiatives – the assessment policy, literacy across the curriculum or whatever it happens to be. They will feel accountable to the head teacher for meeting daily and weekly targets that squeeze work out of the staff. Having less teaching reduces the status of teaching in their list of important daily routines. The less teaching they do, the more distant their memory of the stress and the massive drain of energy that 'back to back' teaching in poorly motivated classes brings the staff. They are guilty of forgetting just how hard it is to teach all day and, for their part, the classroom teachers constantly underestimate how complex managing a difficult school can be. Both sides tend to romanticise the position of the other. The senior manager wishes for a good old-fashioned lesson to teach, away from the constant demands of the head teacher. The regular classroom teacher fantasises about only teaching one period a day and standing around chatting to other staff in the school office with a cup of tea.

Senior managers are inclined, through forgetfulness of earlier careers, to be ultra critical of classroom teachers who don't meet deadlines from senior agendas, forgetting the long hours that preparing lessons and marking books takes outside of the school day. Similarly, the teachers forget how time-consuming it can be to see an angry parent, to write an invigilation timetable or to investigate an incident of assault on a member of staff.

In a difficult school the gap between the teachers who teach most of the time and the senior managers who teach some of the time is narrower. The senior managers will have to do a tremendous amount of fire-fighting to support colleagues in the classroom. They will inevitably spend much of their non-contact time being called to break up an emergency or defuse a confrontation. So, although they have less than a one-to-thirty pupil–teacher ratio faced by their colleagues, they do inherit the most explosive and seriously disturbed pupils who have often instigated difficulties that become emotionally draining to unravel.

So there is a natural tension between the teachers and senior managers in a difficult school. Each set suspects that the other is 'skiving'. One is having an easy life not having to teach loads of crazy classes, and one is having a simple life only attending to their own classroom and not the 'spill-overs' from everyone else. Senior managers become aggravated because they feel that many colleagues stir up needless confrontations – which they have then to quell – fail to meet basic deadlines, arrive late to lessons and don't do enough marking.

Middle managers and teachers feel that they are often left unsupported in difficult situations and that senior staff should spend less time in their offices and more in the corridors.

Interestingly, when inspections take place in difficult schools, both sides prove each other right. The head and deputies are out pacing the corridors and maintaining an unusually high profile and the teachers are on time to classes, meet deadlines, plan lessons in writing, mark books and try to avoid confrontations. In the normal daily run of events, neither side can keep this up.

How senior management can help you in a difficult school

Understand their basic psychology before you can appreciate what you can get out of them. They may not be dealing with fights, blow-outs and emergencies in your classroom every second of the day, but they will be busier doing this than senior colleagues in easier schools. The volume of emergencies leave them with less time than other senior managers to think, plan and administer, so they are very stressed. The volume of crisis referral means that logical stepped progression of certain offences leading to definite penalties, such as temporary or permanent exclusion, cannot take place. Even a short-term exclusion needs the permission of the head, a typed letter and a time-consuming readmission interview. Difficult schools have a huge swathe of difficult pupils who are constantly offending in serious ways. But the difficult school is trying to pretend that it is improving so much that it is like any normal school. There is pressure on it to believe its own PR and so a higher rate of temporary and permanent exclusion is never going to be the answer. Put bluntly, the senior management do not have the time, energy or the overall inclination to exclude pupils a lot of the time. The problem names will simply 'swill' around in the system, being passed back and forth.

As it is a 'no-win' situation at this level, it is best to only seek heavy-duty back-up on rare occasions and you should have commanding evidence at your disposal about what you have done to try to solve that problem pupil's behaviour in the past. Show them how you have contacted parents, seen parents, referred the problem through the correct middle-management system and they cannot avoid rewarding you by giving some help. Prove to them that you have followed the key 'difficult school' maxim, 'inhaled your own smoke' and they will be predisposed to back you up firmly and effectively.

Without this regular trade-off you will establish 'negative' relations with them, bringing them only problems which you never really try to solve or be flexible about. Difficult schools choke on their daily dose of problems and can breathe a little more freely if responsibility is taken for trying to handle them at all levels and in a 'hotch potch' of ways. This involves 'muddling through' and 'turning a blind eye' to some pupils and their families for much of the time in order to survive.

You will also establish yourself as a respected member of staff in senior management's books if you do all your paperwork on time. One of their biggest stresses comes from chasing up staff who ignore administrative deadlines.

Practical help to look for at senior management level

1 Like middle managers, they can remove troublemakers from your room.
2 They can help and support you as you try to settle a class down.
3 They can help you detain a difficult group of pupils at the end of a morning or afternoon session.

4 They can speak to a whole class, making the case for the school expectations of good behaviour to back you up. (Be careful how you use them in this respect as it doesn't help you if they impose their authority on a group and, as they leave, the trouble starts again.) It is helpful, however, if their intervention calms the class down long enough to allow you to gain lesson momentum for yourself.

5 They can internally exclude students from all lessons or some lessons or put them on a personal report to the senior manager or head of year.

6 They can see parents on your behalf or alongside you.

7 They can make the case for a temporary exclusion from school to the head.

8 They can put pressure on the head of department to give you more help.

9 They can speed up the process of special needs support getting into your classroom or the situation whereby a pupil can be withdrawn.

10 They can encourage a head of department to change the groupings of their sets to relieve pressure on you. They can get heads of year to alter form groupings if certain mixtures of students in one group are proving difficult to you and other teachers.

11 If they are effective and experienced classroom practitioners, they can give you some useful tips about classroom management in an informal way.

12 They can push hard to get you useful in-service training quickly. This could be watching and learning from good practice internally or going on useful courses.

13 Cover is likely to be the province of one or more than one senior manager and they may be able to keep your name off it, at a time of day or during a part of the week when you have very stressful lessons.

14 They can shield you from the anger and aggression of very difficult parents when you have done something professionally dubious.

15 They can be concerned and supportive in the most general sense, praising you when you do something well, and boosting your confidence when you feel demoralised about the pupils' behaviour and are inclined to blame yourself. If you feel constructive and good about your relationship with them, it will help you through difficult times.

16 Positive relations with senior managers are useful as they regularly meet with the head to tell him or her what is happening in the school. If they see you as an effective performer, it might help to forward your career.

17 If you feel negative towards your managers and don't get on with them, it will add to your tension and stress levels which are probably already high enough.

18 A good senior manager is a major asset to your survival in a 'difficult school'. Indeed, what senior managers do behind the scenes in terms of planning, evaluating and implementing education policy is vital to whether a difficult school stays difficult, gets significantly easier or becomes totally unbearable.

The singularly most important help that the head and senior managers give to you is to have a sound educational philosophy behind which they can get the whole staff to work solidly as a team. As this book emphasises on many occasions, it is by working as a team that teachers can begin to combat so many problems just a little bit more easily. If you are trying to push a grand piano up a hill, your only chance of 'success' is to get all available personnel to cooperate!

BUILDING RELATIONSHIPS WITH NON-TEACHING STAFF

Meal supervisors

As a teacher, you may volunteer to help out on the break and lunch duties of the week.

A queue in a dining room is one of the hottest spots in the school day. Unless you work in an incredibly calm school, these queues can quickly resemble an angry mob on the first day of the January sales, with a sea of bodies pushing and shoving.

Whether you stagger lunch hours or let your many pupils off site to ease the pressure on your dining facilities, there always seem to be too many pupils trying to pass through the canteen.

Meal supervisors often try and demand the highest standards of behaviour from the pupils, far greater in their levels of insistence than teachers in a lesson. Indeed, they seem to despise large parts of the teaching staff, including some or all of the senior managers for their lax liberal standards. But their demand for good manners often backfires because they do not have the moral authority that comes from the positive relationships with pupils that teachers build in the classroom. So whereas most teachers understand that the 'squaddie manner' doesn't work, some supervisors charge into confrontation, trading insults with the pupils.

Unfortunately when things go wrong, the meal staff expect the teacher to bail them out. And they don't respect your right to be off duty that moment, trying to have your own short lunch break in peace, dragging you away from your mouthful, to get stuck into a shouting match. In fact they are more likely to engineer a confrontation, when they see you around.

Working with the lunch staff

1 Be nice to them and have a chat about things, in those quiet moments on the lunch duty when everybody is relaxed.
2 Explain to individual supervisors, who constantly expect you to reinforce their authority, that you are not always on duty and are sometimes just getting your

lunch. Therefore they should leave you alone, unless there's a real emergency.

3 Don't get drawn on the subject of pupils' terrible manners and behaviour. It's an invitation to a long commentary on how teachers are parents aren't strict enough, young people don't respect their elders and things weren't like this when they were at school. Given some of the meal supervisors are my age or younger, I know that the golden age to which they fondly refer, never existed. I also appreciate that many of them truanted school themselves in their last years or now seem to have children at this school or others, getting into lots of trouble. They tell you this when they are feeling relaxed, but forget it when they have just had a confrontation with a pupil in the lunch queue. But it's not worth arguing with them, instead quietly note how intolerant one set of adults are of the shortcomings of many of their own younger generation of sons, daughters and nephews.

Strategies for controlling queues of pupils, especially lunch queues

- If the queue starts in an orderly calm way, it's far easier to keep it like that. But if it's not supervised in the first couple of minutes and gets to be a seething mass of bodies, you will find it very hard to get order again. Get there on time.
- Ninety five per cent of pupils will queue in a fair 'first come, first served' way, if there is order. Five per cent will try and queue jump. They will mainly be silly boys. If you stop them and ensure that they go to the back of the queue, everybody else will feel that justice has been done and will cooperate in adjusting the queue, if asked to.
- If you arrive when the queue has got off to a bad start and is a mass of pushing bodies, the best intervention

you can make is to form a human barrier, by stepping somewhere into the middle and regulating the flow of people past you from that position. This won't be perfect but it will help restore some order for the lunch staff at the front of the scrum.

- If the situation isn't going well, meal supervisors will immediately request your support. Whereas, if you weren't there, they would find a way of sorting out the situation for themselves.

The premises team

Previously known as the school caretakers, some primary schools only have one who lives on the site. Big secondary schools could have a team of three of four people.

They are absolutely vital to the smooth running of the school, not just in school hours but for all the extended community use some primary and secondaries have. As a teacher, you need to call upon them in all kinds of urgent situations where their swift intervention will save you from protracted crowd control problems.

- A child has vomited all over the desk in the middle of the lesson.
- A pigeon is trapped in the stair well next to your class room and pupils have gathered around, causing it to flap around in a state of panic.
- A window has been broken in a classroom door and there's jagged glass everywhere.
- Somebody has let off a stink bomb outside your classroom.
- You have been so flustered that you've written on a whiteboard in indelible ink.

This is a list of just some of the things they do, that make or break the good order of a school. Like the meal supervisors, the premises team are often very confrontational and 'macho' with the pupils. It is not surprising that they find them irritating, when you consider the list of jobs I've just mentioned that they are regulary asked to respond to. They also bemoan the golden age when the pupils behaved respectfully and did not grafitti, spit on stairs, drop chewing gum on the new carpet and flick cigarette butts behind the bike sheds. Yet in those unguarded moments, they tell you how they personally did almost all of them when they were larking around at school and got caned good and proper for it!

How to get the best out of the premises staff

1 Be pleasant and polite. Give them plenty of warning of the jobs that you want them to do.
2 Consult them about the best way of doing something and try and come up with compromises that minimise hard work for them, whenever possible.

Working with the inspectors

Inspectors come and visit you in the school from the Local Authority and Central Government. They need to be treated with extreme caution. If we lived in an educational world where there was open dialogue, inspectors would be trusted to take the truth back to the educational masters about the real challenges facing your School and how you are dealing with them. But telling inspectors the truth is a dangerous recipe for any teacher who doesn't want to get themselves and their head teacher into a lot of trouble. Unfortunately, the majority of inspectors will twist any weaknesses you admit to and then blame them on you or the management in your school – so what's wrong will become your fault! This encourages Heads and senior teams to 'spin positively' at any opportunity and put on a never ending 'good show' to external audiences. The system of punitive inspection encourages you to 'talk up' rather than 'talk about' problems.

How to handle inspectors effectively

1 Be polite and attentive. Frame your comments positively. Give everything you are in charge of 'the sun ray treatment'. So something that clearly isn't working is described in terms of ' it would be even better if'.
2 Prepare yourself carefully for an inspector's visit, in the same way as you would for a job interview. Think through what you have done and find the evidence for it. Practice describing all your work in a very positive light as it is always the case that glass is described as 'half full' and not 'half empty'.
3 Give the inspectors paper records of the progression of any initiative you have been involved in. They love documentation that justifies what you are saying.
4 Don't ever complain about the inefficiency of other organisations, agencies or individuals. Honest evaluation of the work of others could bounce back on you.
5 Getting a good inspection report always reinforces your position as an effective teacher. A bad report will lead to inevitable questions about your efficiency and will not help your standing in the school.

Chapter 10

Being a tutor in a rough school

You are almost certainly going to be given a tutor group unless you are appointed into a pastoral middle management role. The rougher the school, the more significant this job is and therefore the more stressful and timeconsuming!

THE CONTEXT

As always, tough schools will talk about the role of a tutor in a way which suggests that the job is the same as it is in the leafy suburbs and shires. The basic parallel is that a normal tutor group in an inner-city school will be as difficult as the forms they assign to the most experienced and established teachers in an ordinary comprehensive. The hard groups are 'off the Richter scale' in terms of their huge numbers of difficult characters, truants and latecomers.

Since my first writing this book, most schools have passed the process of chasing absence to administrative staff in the school office. This has improved the working conditions for form tutors, who are no longer expected to write all the letters and make all the routine phone calls about pupil absence in their tutor group.

But tutors still see their form groups every day and are the first port of call for discussions about poor punctuality and attendance. Subject teachers rely on them to support their efforts to challenge poor behaviour and lack of effort in lessons around the school. If you become an effective tutor, you are pulled into a series of extensive running dialogues with pupils and their parents , even if you no longer do routine administration around attendance and punctuality.

Tutoring in tough schools can be frustrating. Pupils don't always turn up to registration. There are at least two or three persistent truants in an average tutor group of 25 and between three and ten pupils who will truant an afternoon here and a day there unless you are 'on their backs' all the time. These tutor groups are often unstable due to high mobility, with students leaving to go to a 'better' school when a place comes up and excluded pupils from other schools trying to get in to replace them. There is the casual intake of pupils who are new to the country or new to the area. They often bring a whole host of language and attendance problems with them.

In general, the parents' relationships with the phone companies are variable. Mobile phone lines are constantly being cut off and reconnected. Similarly, there is a high percentage of temporary accommodation, and addresses are often outdated. So it is difficult to contact the parents about difficulties their children are experiencing at school, and probably also at home. Obviously, as the teacher usually has a lack of time, the above difficulties can put all but the resiliently determined tutors off contacting parents at home. Nevertheless you, the tutor, are supposed to be the first and regular point of call on behaviour, attendance and punctuality matters.

METHODS OF DEALING WITH PUNCTUALITY AND ATTENDANCE

Statistical research documented in many studies has questioned the degree of difference an individual school policy can make to attendance and punctuality. To a large extent, the level of absenteeism and lateness is a direct reflection of the community the school serves and of the parents' interest and commitment to education. However, as tutor in a difficult school you can and do make a difference in very practical ways to attendance and punctuality for your group. For example, in my tutor group of twenty-two, only nine attend regularly with very good time-keeping. Theoretically I am supposed to have a goal of 90 per cent attendance and punctuality. In practice, I score between 70 and 85 per cent on attendance and about 55 to 70 per cent on punctuality. But when I am away, the whole attendance and punctuality of my tutor group to school plummets. On a daily basis I have great difficulty persuading some of my tutor group to sit down and listen to me during registration, but a supply teacher cannot even get them all into the room. Many of the group realise that I am not there and immediately truant. As a tutor, then, it is probably impossible to achieve national norms in your group, even if you try to do your job brilliantly.

But if you don't make a real effort to make an issue out of punctuality and attendance, figures really dive. So your positive work is essentially the avoidance of the negative that is to say, 'complete chaos'.

METHODS OF INCREASING PUNCTUALITY AND ATTENDANCE

Pupils don't come to school, or are persistently late for negative reasons. Rewarding will offer a positive solution to a negative situation.

Do's

1 Reward those who are not late and come on time. It is not just something to be taken for granted.

2 Praise them verbally and use something such as the smiley face stamp in their contact books or on a tutor group rewards chart for punctuality and attendance. Hopefully this can tie in with whole school rewards that get presented in assemblies.

3 Establish a simple routine for these rewards and stick to it. It is something for which pupils need daily and weekly reminders. Try to set your small rewards at a level which the majority, rather than the minority, have a chance of reaching.

4 Phone parents to discuss their son's or daughter's lateness. This is more effective than holding long detentions. Explain to the parents that lateness, like attendance, is something you can refer to the Education Welfare services. Attendance and lateness are issues for which parents have a legal responsibility. This is, at the very least, something you have the right to 'hassle' them about.

5 If you decide to have short detentions for lateness, have them on the day that the lateness occurs.

6 Some pupils respond well to being put on a report for lateness and punctuality monitoring. Getting good grades on this lesson by lesson and day to day seems to give them short-term goals with which they can motivate themselves.

7 As a teacher and a tutor learn to be realistic. Some pupils are so disruptive and negative about their schooling that having them in registration and lessons is counter-productive. If they are not there, thank your lucky stars!

8 On the other hand, by sitting with a pupil and discussing his or her lateness and poor attendance sympathetically and constructively, you may uncover some underlying problems that you may be able to resolve.

Don'ts

Lateness and poor attendance are negatives. Responding with negatives generally reinforces rather than cures them.

1 Don't get into a mass punishment syndrome of long detentions over lateness. The theory that pupils will hurry along to school on time just because they are scared of being kept back in their own time just doesn't work – even though it seems logical.
2 Punishing pupils who don't want to attend school is entirely counter-productive. Be grateful if they attend, but are late every day. Take things one small step at a time.
3 Don't waste too much of your time phoning, letter writing and reporting to the EWO about pupils who have been through that process many times before and who may come in for a few days before 'knocking off' again. There are more productive ways of spending your precious time.
4 Don't get demoralised by the Ofsted claims that a school must be failing if it has less than 90 per cent attendance. Some schools can be trying their hardest with every conceivable good strategy but the pupil attendance sticks at 80 to 85 per cent.

THE ROLE OF TUTOR IN A ROUGH SCHOOL

As a tutor, your role of holding pupils back at the end of the day and discussing their progress and problems with their subject teachers is crucial. You are often able to fill in other staff on family circumstances that might explain current difficulties in the classroom. At the heart of your relationship with students in a difficult inner-city tutor group is the consistency of your relations with them. You are there for them twice a day and inevitably in those registrations impromptu and informal conversations take place. They get used to you and vice versa. They know that you will talk to their parents over the phone and call them in. You have done it before. But they rely on their tutor to look after their bags and coats for them during the school day and let them into your room at inconvenient times to get them. They also know that you will listen longer to them in situations where other teachers may not, because you are their tutor. If any bits of the PSHE programme have worked they might have a slightly personal insight into you and you into them.

But, above all, familiarity and consistency of approach will give confidence and be an emotional backbone. In hard schools, teachers are always changing and there are always loads of supply teachers. This would destabilise any school but it is especially difficult in circumstances where pupils are already short of nurture and regular adult consistency from their home backgrounds. This is the essential role of tutors – to be there every day to show that they have a commitment to the individuals in their tutor group. You will let them have their say. As their tutor you know their good and bad sides from regular viewing and they have gone through the long process of getting used to you. It has often been a painful and frustrating process for both sides. But tutors who have been tried and tested and won through, have an important status with their group, between that of 'parent' and 'teacher'.

Consistency and becoming established

The importance of consistency and becoming established over a duration is very important in the rough inner city school. Whether as a teacher or as a tutor, if you battle on, you will find the pupils come to accept you and give you an easier time. The first year is the hardest but by the end of the second it begins to get easier. This is true for your first teaching job in any school, but it is magnified tenfold in a school with a difficult catchment area.

Obviously you must face the fact that the struggle you will have is immense and protracted. Many teachers just cannot cope with the level of aggression and non co-operation to which they are subjected. They choose to leave these types of schools quite quickly. It is likely, therefore, that the pupils are slightly surprised if they test you with a lot of aggravation and you do pull through. In tough schools, the turnover of staff is higher than in easier ones and is a sign of the pressure that teachers work under. Another frequent feature is the high number of temporary teachers filling many jobs because the school has been unable to make a stable full-time appointment due to lack of suitable applicants. The irony of this situation is that the children who need the most security and stability make it so difficult for so many of their teachers that they leave.

Chapter 11

Verbal abuse and fighting among the pupils

This is essentially a chapter on the singularly most frequent symptoms of low motivation and low self-esteem among the pupils – insulting and inciting each other, known as 'cussing', and having fights, or 'set piece spectaculars'.

WHERE DOES THE AGGRESSIVE CULTURE COME FROM?

The verbal and physical abuse are a core part of school culture amongst young teenagers. It is a culture that society and the media encourage, whilst pretending to condemn. The English football match is typical. Players verbally and physically abuse each other on the pitch and fans brawl off it. Despite decrying hooliganism, there is a fascination in the media for gang rivalry off the pitch and players' power struggles on it. Similarly, wrestling and boxing are mass media sports in which size, aggression and violence are glorified.

Hollywood has aggression and violence at the core of many of its storylines. There are whole genres of film with the super macho hero. There are hundreds of film narratives where heroes assert their moral integrity by fighting violence with violence, abuse with abuse. The goodie wins by beating up and killing the baddie in a superior demonstration of machismo. The audience is taken along with this scenario – we are willing the goodie to teach the baddie a lesson and get revenge.

What are boys and girls supposed to make of all the constant glorification of physical powers, aggression and violence (the emotional and physical consequences of which are never shown)?

What are they supposed to make of the constant use of violence for entertainment? What are they supposed to deduce from the paucity of emotional expression from many male role models surrounding them, other than endless demonstrations of puffed-up aggression and rage.

In challenging secondary schools many pupils are both fascinated and fearful of physical violence. But they expect it to surround them as a part of school life in the playgrounds, corridors and roads that lead to and from their School and the local housing estates. Here is a description of the common themes of that pupil culture.

The key features of Macho Culture.

- You have to fight to defend your honour. Maintaining honour goes beyond verbal negotiations.
- Looking after your Mum's reputation comes before even your own.
- Violence is entertaining.
- Violence gains status.
- Retribution and revenge for a perceived slight are far more important than any possible school based consequences, such as detention or exclusion.
- Having an uncontrollable temper is something people can be proud of.
- Males don't show any emotion, except anger and rage.

CUSSING

'Cussing' or 'telling' is a complex matter and takes place at a number of levels from the silly and trivial to the deeply upsetting. The context, that is to say, the relationship between the antagonists, the sexes involved and the situation in which it occurs, must all be taken into account before you, the teacher, decide how to handle it most effectively.

Its school context

Cussing matters because it is a perpetual irritant to the process of trying to teach and a constant 'attention' block in those trying to learn. In a survey conducted in a difficult inner-city secondary, the male and female pupils agreed that it was the one issue that accounted for more distraction, aggression and violence between pupils than anything else. Cussing predominantly occurs boy on girl and boy on boy, but the same contexts and terminologies are used by girls on other girls. Of course, it can also be turned on you or any member of the staff in certain situations.

Types of cussing

Cussing takes many forms.

Sexist

The most common form, sexist cussing, has at its centrepiece abuse around 'Your Mum'. Boys' mothers are sacred to them in an exterior culture where fathers are often absent from daily life. There is the most elaborate and detailed subculture of 'mother cussing'. The general cuss for the boy is to suggest that another pupil's mother has easy sexual virtue. So the boast will often be made that Mum has been sexually exploited or abused in some way.

The size, shape or 'humanness' of mothers is called into question in the 'Your Mum' culture. Abuse ranges from light and jokey to grossly obscene and pornographic.

At all levels the 'Your Mum' culture denigrates women. Typical examples of lurid imagery are: 'I had your Mum last night. She looks so rough that I put a bag over her head' or 'Your Mum has got four legs and a tail.' Using just the entree of 'Your Mum!' and nothing more can be incitement enough to start a fight. Both sexes accuse each other of 'gayness' and sexual deviancy. One of the most vicious cusses is for one boy to goad another for homosexuality. Boys cuss girls for being lesbians, as do other girls. However, as most sexist cussing denigrates women, the girls often respond to sexist abuse from boys by attacking their intellect and socio-economic potential in society as a male. For example, referring to the size of a boy's brain or the fact that he cannot read well or that he is going to grow up a car thief or a mugger. Cussing deals in a slagging interchange of stereotypes.

Racist

The racist cuss is more complicated in the life of mixed racial inner-city schools. White versus black racism will go undercover in a multi-racial setting with white pupils 'thinking' rather than saying it on many occasions. Black pupils, however, will regularly taunt each other with 'racist' cusses about the 'blackness' or 'African-ness' of other pupils. Between black pupils, it is claimed that this kind of 'needling' is just good humoured. But there obviously is a deeper level to this language of self-abuse which, as a teacher in a rough school, you need to study further. What you can be sure of is that 'cussing' about blackness does cause great tension and offence and will therefore destabilise your relationship with pupils in and out of lessons. It also encourages poor self-images among many black pupils. For example, black girls often stereotype black boys as being worthless and only capable of thieving and imprisonment.

Sizist

Sizist cussing has other clear links to sexism. Boys cuss the girls as being 'fat', 'skinny' and vice-versa. Boys make comments about the shape and size of girls' breasts and girls cuss back in self-defence – often about boys' sexual organs.

There is a tendency for the boys to attack the girls in a mixed school and for them to try to defend themselves.

Materialist/personal characteristics

Cussing takes the form of using another pupil's socioeconomic circumstances to denigrate them. Comments on their clothes, hair and shoes are brought up. Their lack of 'designer labels' is talked of. They are told they are dirty and shouldn't touch anyone else. They are reminded that they live in poverty and squalor.

THE IMPACT OF CUSSING

Pupils often save their most colourful language for 'cussing'. It is rich in adjectives and imagery and fantastic in its imagination. If such imagination and skills were used to enrich their own curriculum it would totally transform their language work and studies. But it is an alternative culture used to block the smooth running of the official lessons of the school. It is a constant irritant in and out of the classroom where pupils become engrossed in a 'cussing' dialogue instead of writing or listening to the teacher. It is the most common cause of fights in and out of lessons and school.

'Chinese whispers' inflate the consequence of the standard cuss. A friend tells another friend what someone has said about him or her. The 'cuss' is magnified out of all proportion and the serious trouble begins.

The 'cussing' syndrome is the equivalent of pouring petrol on a fire. It is a form of verbal bullying and intimidation but it ranges from mild to very severe. All schools have it, but it is rampant, regular and 'up front' in difficult schools. As a teacher you'll have to deal with it constantly, and if you fail to conquer it, it will completely destabilise your lessons. And don't think it cannot be turned on you. Teachers of both sexes can be the victim of sizist, sexist and racist abuse. If you are a man you could be called bald, short, spindly, fat, grey or gay! If you are female, you could be at the receiving end of repeated comments about your hair, breast, bum and clothes. For many teachers who are already feeling vulnerable about any, or indeed all, of these aspects of their appearance, their personal confidence is destroyed when it is needed to be at its most ebullient in a difficult classroom.

I have heard of the constant harassment of women teachers with comments about the hair under their arms or their 'moustaches'. Others minimise risk of insult by covering themselves from head to toe, never changing their basic hairstyle or limited repertoire of school clothes for fear of a surge in 'cussing' in their classes.

Teachers are, of course, human beings and the personal comments muttered under the breath or shouted out loud in the chaos of a difficult lesson do strike home to hurt and irritate, despite the obvious need for professionalism to rise above it all. Of course pupils can also be incredibly complimentary about a hair-cut or a new pair of trousers, but many teachers will be too scared to risk it.

STRATEGIES FOR DEALING WITH CUSSING

1 Understanding what it is and the various forms that it takes.

2 Understanding the context and the nuance in which you hear it take place. As a teacher in a rough school you are seeking to avoid confrontation, so it is important to judge when to take on 'cussing' and when to ignore it. For example, in certain contexts in which certain pupils are involved, a series of cusses could quickly lead to a fight which will finish your lesson completely. In another circumstance, the cussing is relatively 'gentle' and you would be best to make a joke to stop it happening. On another occasion that relatively 'gentle' game of insulting could be used in a ruthless campaign of intimidation. You must assess the personnel and the balance of forces of those involved in the general 'cussing' going on. Sometimes you should intervene and with great moral force, whatever the consequences on a lesson.

3 As a general rule you must work on the medium- and long-term strategy of eliminating it from your classroom. It is, at best, a low-level irritant and gets in the way of pupils' concentration and learning. You will be most effective if the school places a high premium on a 'whole school' attack on it.

4 Having open discussion with a class about why certain words are hurtful and provocative, will give you the chance to work out the dynamic of the group and its relationships. In some classes, they are playing with the conventions of 'cussing' and, in others, serious bullying is taking place. You need to open up the debate on the issue as far as you can so that pupils are not surprised if you try to prevent it happening. Quite often the 'cussing' is simply a group technique for irritating you during your own lesson.

5 Find out how other colleagues deal with it. Is there a whole school approach which the pupils expect you to adopt? Is there a colleague who deals with it in a way that you could copy?

6 Involve parents, heads of department and heads of year when you are concerned.

7 Contact parents and don't be afraid to 'shame' the pupils by repeating exactly what was said to you, even if it is embarrassing. The parents will often be shocked by the grim detail of the insult, which will be more effective than just telling them that their son or daughter had been personally abusive to you.

Don'ts

1 Don't ignore cussing completely.

2 Don't try to stamp on it with firm and powerful rebukes whenever you hear it. This would be a recipe for continual confrontation.

3 Don't try to stifle all discussion about it within the class.

4 Don't feel that you cannot refer to other colleagues for help.

5 Don't suffer it in isolation, especially when it has been turned on you. However personally abusive or embarrassing the taunts have been, you must get help from colleagues to challenge them.

6 Don't forget that insults directed at other pupils can quickly be turned on you. If you can discourage pupils doing it to each other, they will be more likely to leave you alone.

7 Don't forget that pupils are experimenting with language and adult imagery when they cuss. There is an educational role in what sometimes seems like personal, hurtful, malicious sexual abuse. In particular, it can be interpreted as a rather clumsy form of flirtation and exploration. Try to stay calm and disentangle, where possible, the lighter experimental banter from aggressive sexist abuse.

SET PIECE SPECTACULARS

Fights (individual and group) 'steaming' and 'happy slaps'

In lessons, corridors and breaktimes you are going to be called upon to intervene in fights. Rough schools have them regularly. They are often caused by 'cussing' and other forms of bullying that have taken place within school. They can often be the produce of a quarrel between families that spills over from the local housing estate. They usually involve two protagonists but can involve a group of individuals fighting or attacking another pupil. They are especially dangerous when they involve 'strangers' who are not at the school but have come on to the site on a violent errand.

They can start spontaneously in playground conditions where too many pupils are pushing through a narrow point in the corridor. The only quarrel being someone accidentally hurting someone else by standing on their toes. Or a group of pupils who are pushing and shoving playfully, but have the intention to start a general disorder.

The last type of behaviour can take a more serious and premeditated form, that of 'steaming' or 'rushing'. This is where a massive group of individuals decide to jump on another pupil. It is usually done as a 'laugh' rather than with 100 per cent malicious intent, but it is very dangerous as the individuals involved lose their personal responsibility for what damage they cause as the general morass takes place. Forty pupils may jump on another and begin kicking that person for no obvious reason. It is similar to a mob lynching and the victim can be very seriously hurt in this situation. Another variant of 'steaming' is one tutor group against another. Again, it usually starts as half-serious skirmishes but under the general silliness of 'hoofing around' individuals can really get hurt. Steaming is very different to fighting or 'beating up' – the very lack of personal execution of malicious intent gives it no proper confines. For example, X punches Y within the expected remit situation of a fight, then X, Y and Z, along with ten others begin, for a laugh, to kick wildly at a victim who is on the floor or is pushed into a corner. They don't know the damage they have done or the limitations on how far they can go.

Happy slaps

Happy slapping has been a variant on 'steaming' and a new craze sweeping school corridors and playground in many secondary schools, in the last twelve months. It is phenomenon that looks set to stay and mutate, as the years go by.

New technology has brought new problems of violence and disorder. Third Generation Phones that can take, then send violent video clips are the rage. If you are a teacher out on patrol in the corridors, then you may well have had to break up a 'happy slapping' maelstrom. The scrap or school fight you used to deal with, is now a media event, with an audience around the whole school and potentially through E mailing images, an event right across the local area, the whole of London and the country.

The standard format is a slap round the head. The perpertrator gets another pupil to video it. If the 'happy slap' is a planned event, there is likely to be a huge crowd emerging from the woodwork, out of classrooms from along the corridor. This is down to the new technology again. 'Blue Tooth', an infra red system, can send video nasties from one phone to another, through ceilings and classroom walls within a ten metre radius. Providing both users have the system, it's free of charge. As the 'happy slap' is beamed from one screen to another, the corridors will fill up. As you wade your way through the crowd, the press pack of observers hold their phone cameras out and there's a frenzy of snapping.

THE ROLE OF THE TEACHER IN A FIGHT SITUATION

As a teacher your biggest problem in a fight situation is not the fight itself but the role of bystanders, spectators and semi-involved participants. In rough schools, pupils will react in one of several ways when two pupils are fighting. They will form a 'ringside' and bunch around the individuals to watch. Sometimes the ringside is hostile to any attempts to break up the action, hoping that the combatants will get a real good chance to smash the hell out of each other. In particular cases there is a real 'blood lust' in the watching mob. On other occasions, there is a combination of shock, fear and fascination at the violence and anger of one or both the fighters and the crowd is literally frozen to the spot. This kind of fight can often be very difficult and dangerous break up without a lot of support.

Often fights are much more 'benign' than this and the honour of both protagonists will be satisfied if they can sling a few ritual punches at each other before being pulled apart. They are almost waiting for an intervention, relieved if it comes before either is hurt. In this situation the mob can be an ally and there will often be pupils who will help you to restrain one or both would-be fighters.

Remember that in 'tough' schools there is a rank order for 'fighters' which probably extends through a first to a third division. There is often a controlling clique in a school and, within that, the gang leader. On the whole you won't be breaking up their fights as they haven't needed to fight since the first year to prove themselves. Fights often occur among the second and third division 'pretenders', trying to push their status up within the rank order. If there was a real fight involving the controlling clique, it would probably be both unusual and vicious – the 'quashing' of a new competing interest. This is very rare as 'promising young turks' are usually absorbed into the number one gang, rather than conquered.

As a teacher you would find it to your advantage to 'suss out' who the 'controllers' are. I made a study of them in one of the school in which I worked. They are seldom the rudest and most disruptive pupils when left alone, but trying to challenge their status by ordering them to move to lessons at the end of lunchtime or by breaking up a fight they want to see continued, will lead to public humiliation for you, the teacher. It is possible for key members of this clique to be simultaneously striving hard and 'intelligently' in lessons while organising mugging and extortion from younger pupils in and around the school.

STRATEGIES FOR HANDLING FIGHTS

1 Act on the basic premise that prevention is always better than cure. Stopping a fight before it starts is always easier than breaking one up.
2 Read and react to signals that indicate a fight is about to break out. Body language, the build up of a crowd of people following each other or chasing through the corridors or playground of a school.
3 Assess the scale of the crowd disturbance and only go it alone if you feel comfortable. It is usually possible to break up a fight with some humour or calming body language and words. This kind of action is most effective before blows are exchanged and pain and honour must be defended. Calmness has less effect on inflamed tempers once the action has begun.
4 In fight situations involving a gang onto one – intruders attacking a pupil – you would be foolish if you didn't think of your own safety. Run to get help or send a pupil you know you can trust. You have no status with an intruder and this renders you as helpless and as vulnerable as the victim. Police are probably needed urgently.

5 In some situations none of the pupils will help you. Don't waste time recriminating with them, just run and get the nearest help.

6 Accept the fact that you could get punched and kicked in a fight situation, either by the protagonists or by someone behind you in the crowd. Don't lose your temper and lash out. Back off, withdraw and go and get help.

7 You have the right to act as a parent might in a dangerous situation to protect the safety of a pupil or pupils, but actually holding onto or prising pupils apart is a very grey area legally. When in doubt, don't do it. Remember: if you hold one pupil, you might unintentionally be helping another to kick or hit an intended victim.

8 If you can prevent a fight by restraining a pupil, then do so, but do it in such a way that it constitutes minimal physical force and cannot be interpreted as an assault.

9 Your 'street cred' with the pupils will go up a lot if you show yourself to be calm and resourceful in a fight situation. Many are looking to see if you can be seriously intimidated. They will consider you brave if you 'diffuse' or break up a fight. But knowing this should not encourage you to put yourself at risk. You are employed as a teacher and not as a 'bouncer'.

10 Once fighters are split, take them in opposite directions – one with you and the other with a teacher or a sensible pupil. Isolate them from each other and get statements of what happened.

11 Disperse the crowd. This will be very difficult if you are alone and haven't received back-up from your colleagues. A big crowd in a rough school usually takes a huge team effort to disperse.

12 When it is 'steaming' or 'rushing', urgent back-up is needed from other teachers to call or pull off the

hunting pack before the victim is knocked unconscious or seriously hurt.

13   'Steaming' will stop occurring as a habit if staff can identify the agents provocateurs and ringleaders behind the mob and deal severely with them. A written statement from you about how something started will be useful for senior management.

14   When in doubt, just go for help. It may seem selfish and cowardly if you flee from a situation in which a pupil is being terrorised and hurt but, as in a drowning emergency, no point is served by a person trying to make a rescue in such a hazardous situation as they end up drowning as well!

15   Try to find out which pupils carry status within the school for fighting. If there is a controlling gang within the school, the more you know about it, the better. In difficult situations it could prove to be your ally. In other situations, you will know not to challenge it on your own and it is better to go for help.

Chapter 12

Intrusions and interruptions

QUESTIONNAIRE

How often do outside interruptions impede the progress of your lessons? Look at this list, think of your working day and write down 'F' for frequently, 'O' for occasionally, 'R' for once or twice a year and 'N' for never.

1 Other teachers come into your class and ask you questions or speak to the pupils.
2 Pupils from other classes want to come in and talk to a friend.
3 Pupils are sent to you from other classes for 'bad behaviour'.
4 Pupils from your tutor group try to bring you a problem while you are trying to teach and they are supposed to be in another lesson.
5 Pupils truanting from other classes hang around outside your lesson, disturbing it.
6 Intruding parents come into your room and demand to speak to you about an incident involving their offspring.
7 Intruders come into your room searching for a pupil.
8 Intruders threaten violence on you, if you don't get out of their way.

9 A pupil or pupils you have sent out of your lesson insist on opening the door and shouting into the classroom.

10 Pupils come in late and interrupt the flow of your teaching.

Each of the above has an effect on your lesson momentum. As we have already seen, building lesson momentum is your greatest challenge in a tough school. Consider what affect each type of intrusion has on your ability to 'forward propel' your lesson. How many of these interruptions can occur in the space of one lesson? How do you deal with each kind of interruption?

Intrusions checklist

In a tough school the majority of the above interruptions occur frequently and only the most serious types of violent intrusion would be a very occasional experience. The frequency and seriousness of interruptions depend on a number of factors.

1 Your position in the hierarchy of the school (head of year, head of department, etc.). Status will protect you from some intrusions but give you lots of others.

2 Your position in the building. If you are in or near an unstable curriculum area with lots of supply teachers or struggling regulars, the pupils will be in and out of their rooms constantly.

3 Your position in relation to official entrances to the school. (Most will be kept locked during the day but not all.)

4 Your position in relation to the unofficial entrances to the school. (The low fence, the hole in the fence, etc.)

5 Your position in relations to the 'nooks' and 'crannies' at the ends of corridors or near toilets, where lesson 'bunkers' hang out.

6 The school's effectiveness at intercepting angry parents, and parents without an appointment, who want to see you. This will depend on overall school security and the attitude and vigilance of senior management, office staff and the caretakers.

STRATEGIES FOR DEALING WITH INTERRUPTIONS

Pupils hanging around or truanting

There is no hard and fast rule for dealing with interruptions like this. In a difficult school the corridors become busier as the day progresses. Fewer pupils 'bunk' or get sent out of morning lessons but just before lunch, business picks up and by the afternoon the chance of interruptions is far higher. Some students will never have got to their afternoon lessons and will be hiding in 'dark corners', while others will walk out of their lessons, with or without the permission of their teachers.

Stay calm when dealing with pupils you don't know, who try to 'butt' into your lessons. Persuade them to leave your room, try not to be too confrontational as verbal or physical abuse is always more likely from those you don't know and don't teach. 'Bawling out' a person in front of a large audience is always dangerous.

These kinds of intrusion occur when someone is making an arrangement after school, borrowing or returning money or school equipment or just wanting a chat because they are tired of hanging about in the corridor. They inevitably occur in the first fifteen minutes after a lesson change-over and are very frustrating for a teacher in that they happen simultaneously with that person's attempts to get their own regular pupils to arrive on time, sit down, take coats off and listen.

External intruders

Intruders who are either parents or groups of youths from other schools are a rarer but more dangerous nuisance. You have no quick and easy way of unravelling their problem and what they want is almost certain to cause you 'confrontation' and lose lesson momentum completely. Listen calmly but don't engage in the issue. Steer the angry parent out of the classroom and out of earshot of a class who love to hear their teacher getting 'told' (verbally abused) by another adult. Try to point them in the direction of the school office with a promise to see them when you are not teaching. Get an urgent note to the office via a pupil, warning them of the intrusion. With intruders who are looking for other students but are obviously not their parents, speak politely but urge them to report to the school office or leave the building. Those who come into a school like this are almost always on a 'beating up' errand. Get a message urgently to a senior member of staff as soon as it is safe to do so. If you or members of your class come under attack, try to send a pupil to get help. If this is impossible, try to shout for help and flee from your attacker!

Chapter 13

Time-management in a difficult school

Very few studies have been done of one of the most obvious limiting factors to effective teaching in inner-city classes. The professional time spent out of the classroom affects all secondary school teachers. But in the difficult school this lack of time away from the pupils will spoil the time that teachers *do* have in the classroom.

The average inner-city teacher has to teach for five of the six hours in a working day. They are usually responsible for the pastoral care of a tutor group of pupils. They will usually do a break duty and possibly even a lunch duty once a week. In addition, it is likely that when the school day ends, they will attend at least two meetings a week (subject, pastoral or staff meetings and working parties in some kind of rota). These meetings will usually last until almost 5.00pm. In addition, many teachers will offer lunchtime or extra-curricular activities.

That, therefore, accounts for most of the normal nine-to-five day with a lunch break that would be expected by an office worker with a similar salary. The teachers have longer holidays, but even if we add another hour and a half to their working day, and make it 9.00am to 6.30pm, they still find it almost impossible to deal thoroughly with their wide-ranging responsibilities.

Let's look at those responsibilities in a typical inner-city secondary school. Teachers are supposed to write detailed lesson plans for each lesson they teach. The more difficult the school, the more inspectors press head teachers to check that this is done. Copious lesson planning in writing is seen as a vital ingredient to quell the poor motivation and behaviour in the classroom. Lesson plans must include lesson objectives, resources to be used with particular reference to what, in education, is called differentiated material. In simple terms, this means different pieces of work for the varying abilities of the class. Since the changes to Special Needs provision in schools, lesson plans must show how each individual pupil's special requirement is being targeted by the teacher. Some pupils have a full statement, which might mean they get extra help from a support teacher in some lessons, but the majority of pupils with behaviour or literacy problems are subjected to a massively long-winded bureaucratic process in which they have to prove that they need a full statement. There are five stages of obtaining a statement, and most of these stages place the responsibility for producing extra learning materials, and giving extra individual help, on the already harassed and over-stretched classroom teacher.

There are, however, more elaborate lesson plans, which include strategies for tackling cross-curricular issues such as literacy, numeracy and economic awareness. Many proforma leave a large blank section in which, at the end of the lesson, the teacher should evaluate the general performance.

Let us give serious consideration to the time logistic of filling in these forms properly. In a typical timetable a teacher will need to do this about twenty-five times a week. As most schools have been moving away from broad mixed ability teaching, very few lesson plans can be used twice, unless the teacher has exact parallel classes. Filling in each form takes a minimum of 10 minutes – that is 50 minutes a day filling forms. For some colleagues, the process could take considerably longer.

But a good lesson on paper is no guarantee of a good lesson in the classroom. It is much more important that teachers should think through the lesson they intend to teach a group, in terms of subject content and class management strategies, before there is any value in picking up a planning sheet. They need to gather certain resources for that lesson, which could mean borrowing or preparing afresh several levels of extension work, getting a set of textbooks or a video from a colleague and duplicating materials. The more 'differentiated' the work, the more complex and time consuming is the task is likely to be.

It is very difficult to assess the thinking and organisation time for a lesson in minutes. For a seasoned professional, adhering to something they have taught many times previously, it could be as low as ten minutes per lesson, but on most occasions it will be at least half an hour and even longer if new materials and teaching methods are being piloted. Newly qualified teachers will take at least half an hour to plan the most basic lesson. So we must add yet another 90 minutes to the working day. The average teacher, on current calculations, is working from 9.00am to 5.00pm three times a week, teaching and performing other duties such as supervision, extra clubs and attending meetings. On average, one hour's preparation is gained each day, but at least one of these slots will be lost regularly by sitting in on an absent colleague's class. Actual lesson planning and the writing of lesson plans will take at least another two hours per day. This gives a nine-to-seven working day, and huge areas of a teacher's responsibilities have not yet been included.

Producing lesson materials is a good long-term investment as they can be used again and again. But lesson plans tend to be 'one off' for a particular group of individuals at a particular time. Practical experience shows that the planning process is very individual to each teacher. It is not easy to pick up another teacher's lesson plan and teach effectively from it. Very often it is difficult to use another teacher's lesson materials because what makes perfect sense in the mind of one person as a rationale for a lesson is often hard for another person to penetrate. This is especially true with poorly motivated and badly behaved classes where each teacher has to learn how to 'fight' from the basis of the strongest points in his or her personality and often needs to develop and adapt material as the battle with the class takes place.

What hasn't been timed into the nine-to-seven working day? There has, as yet, been no mention of the marking and assessment through which teachers keep pupils informed of their progress. Marking is a very complex and time-consuming process in all National Curriculum subjects where a lot of student writing is to be read and judged. Inspectors want to see more than a series of red ticks and a comment such as 'Good work, Carol'. Equally, reporting to parents is now a much more long-winded process than it was ten years ago.

An average set of twenty-six exercise books, carefully marked, will involve at least a few alterations to spelling and punctuation. It involves writing a comment of at least two sentences on each book, combining positive praise with some subject-specific suggestions of how the work can be improved. Often there will also be a quality and effort grade, which will take a minimum of 5 minutes per book and, for some teachers, perhaps even longer! The marking of a set of books accounts for almost 90 minutes, and many teachers could have eight or ten different groups of pupils in any week. Teachers in humanities subjects see even more classes as they have less time with each group per week. If schools expect exercise books to be marked at least once every ten working days, then five sets of books each week adds approximately six and a half hours to the nine-to-seven working day. The process of written lesson planning, real lesson planning and marking adds, at least, eleven hours to a teacher's week, beyond the commitment to be with the children in the classroom and colleagues at after-school meetings.

But even this is the tip of the iceberg for ordinary teachers in secondary schools. They are drip fed a process of short reports and profiles for each year group as the academic year goes by. Short reports are usually just a system of grading and a whole set can be done in 45 minutes, but the profiles are very detailed and full of educational jargon. They must take an ordinary teacher at least 10 minutes to write for each pupil, and each teacher will have about 250 a year to do, for all the students they teach. There are two sets of short reports and one set of full profiles per annum.

'Directed time'

The government settled the strikes and industrial action of the early 1980s by introducing a thousand plus hours of 'directed time' where the head of a school could put on meetings, parents evenings and paperwork in addition to the teacher's normal workload of marking and preparation. But the 'directed time' initiative was based on the optimistic and wholly unrealistic view that teachers arrived in time for their first lesson and walked out of school at 3.30pm, empty handed. Only completely idle classroom teachers could behave like this, and in any event they would be unable to perform their basic job descriptions.

Teachers therefore are faced with fitting in 12 hours of work before and after the normal cycles of teaching and attending regular weekly meetings. The whole education system is based on the fallacy that these 12 hours can be used solely for lesson planning and assessment. But the school system has yet more vital managing processes that must be squeezed in. Whatever type of secondary school a teacher is in, he or she will have to deal with the extra labour that comes from building and sustaining good classroom management.

In the leafy middle-class suburbs and the mixed social class comprehensives, controlling lateness, bad behaviour and homework completion through letters home, detentions, interviews with parents and a positive rewards systems may take a token amount of extra time for experienced staff. But in a difficult inner-city secondary school, sustaining the rewards and sanctions systems is vital to the very survival of 90 per cent of the teachers and adds hours to the week. Schools will vary in their effectiveness in backing up individual staff who are combating behaviour difficulties with their classes but, as a general rule, the scale of incidents is so large that all levels of school management tend to get swamped by the number of referrals.

Therefore, individual classroom teachers, while taking all the help on offer, must be realistic and accept that the support they can obtain will never be enough.

Managing the pupils

As we have already outlined, the battle for survival as a teacher in a difficult inner-city school depends on being broad shouldered and resilient enough to 'consume your own smoke'. Teachers must win the control of their own classrooms against the restless and poor academic motivation of many of the pupils. This is a massively time-consuming challenge which is as important as planning lessons carefully and more important than marking books. Interviewing parents, sending letters of complaint and praise, doing detentions every lunchtime and after-school, and using rewards systematically will add at least a further two hours to the working week. The more a teacher does at first, the lower their commitment to it as time passes. But the problems are never wholly conquered even when the majority of pupils have learned to respect the teacher. Dysfunctional, restless, low motivation will return periodically to many individual students irrespective of the number of rewards or sanctions they receive. This is their natural equilibrium when faced with a school system from which, for many complex reasons, they are alienated. As we have discussed previously in this book, these pupils often lack the internal motivation to learn, and have learning and emotional difficulties that schools are poorly equipped to deal with. The process of 'managing' the pupils will consume big chunks of time every week for most teachers!

It would be logical to assume that a hardcore minority of 10–15 per cent of aggressive and disruptive pupils would be permanently excluded from their already hard-pressed schools. But herein lies another great myth of the education system that teachers must face up to if they are to survive in 'difficult' schools. Only a small proportion of these unruly students will be removed. To begin with, no one else would take them, which is probably why they were forced to come to the struggling secondary. Most of them will never commit a serious offence such as attacking a teacher, grievously injuring another pupil or trying to burn down the school, but they will commit a never-ending series of disruptions to the lessons of their fellow pupils over a five-year period. They will persistently fail to do any written work, they will talk while the teacher is trying to explain something to the class, and they will be defiant when reprimanded. They may swear at teachers and other pupils or storm out of the room, but this is not guaranteed to get them final exclusion in a troubled school where such incidents are common. They will be shunted ineffectually around the school system over a long period with parents being called up, letters written, detention served or sometimes missed, the occasional short exclusion and the periodic personal student report to a head of year or tutor. But their behaviour and motivation problems will not be cured and, hourly, they will 'drip-feed' poison into the system. In the past more would have found provision in special units but these have been sacrificed increasingly to education cuts.

The bleak reality for teachers in tough schools is that they have to absorb a high proportion of 'lesson wreckers' every day. When these students combine with a periodically feckless middle ground of pupils and set them off adversely, the scene is set for very difficult and demanding classroom dynamics.

It is perfectly obvious that schools with more than a handful of pupils who fall into this category will struggle to create a purposeful learning environment. But although they would like to exclude more disruptive pupils permanently, they are held in a 'catch 22' situation by educational funding.

These schools are often under-subscribed and trying to raise their roles. Inspectors will be taking a close look at their exclusion rates as a sign of whether the school is winning or losing. Obviously, negative conclusions are drawn when exclusion rates are high. Balanced against this, the under-subscribed schools will be pressurised by their local authorities to take casual admissions, who are often students who have been excluded from other schools in the area. They may have potentially more dangerous track records than the borderline disruptives that the school already has. Schools that are struggling are tightly tied in a no-win situation as regards their recruitment.

TIME COSTING

I have done no time costing on how stressful it is for an ordinary teacher to deal with very difficult classes on a daily basis. Clearly, the pressures on them to plan lessons, create varied teaching materials and mark carefully and regularly are identical to those on colleagues at a 'good' school where the majority of pupils are well motivated. The more difficult a school, the more time is taken up on routine rewarding and punishing, and that applies as much to behaviour management as it does to the normal tasks of teaching (see Table 13.1). But what about the psychological effect of struggling with many classes who are aggressive and poorly motivated? It is not surprising that teachers become demoralised and the quality of their lesson preparation drops. From my time costing, it would seem that even if morale and energy levels remained wholly positive and high, there would still be about 11 or 12 hours of preparation and marking each week as well as several hours devoted to the control of classes. This is not possible, for even the very best of teachers, unless they cut corners in many significant ways!

Table 13.1 Counting up your hours

During any week you will spend time doing the following things	How much time should you spend?	How much time do you spend?
Writing your lesson plans		
Marking and assessing		
Rewarding pupils (certificates, letters home and seeing parents)		
Sanctioning pupils (detentions, letters home, seeing parents and phoning home)		

Discussion points

- Out of the things that you do in a normal working week, what should you spend less time on?
- What must you spend more time on?
- Is it physically possible to do the job that you are asked to do, within a forty hour working week?
- Should you be working more than a forty hour week?
- What role, if any, should holiday time have in a teacher's working time?

PRACTICAL STRATEGIES TO COPE WITH THE 'LACK OF TIME'

Whatever your discussions about the above points have led you to conclude, it is clear that formal and informal demands on a teacher's time in a difficult school will not go away. The reality is that you, the teacher, must learn to find a way to cope with them.

1 You must priorities objectives by learning how to juggle them. One week, sending letters of praise or complaint and interviewing parents takes priority over marking another two sets of books and preparing an extra special lesson. But the following week the priorities must be reversed. Although you must be able to deliver a straightforward teacher-centred lesson using worksheets and textbooks on a regular basis, your survival will be enhanced if you do take risks and experiment with more daring group work and discussion strategies. Using rewards and sanctions carefully and regularly is vital in helping you to establish good classroom relationships, but so is the occasional 'in-depth' marking of a piece of work to enable you to make an accurate assessment of what a pupil can do! Variety means inevitably finding the time for one thing each week at the expense of others, but experimenting with your teaching styles keeps

you and your classes fresh. Occasionally devote most of your extra time to preparing your lessons, and leave the marking. Concentrate only on sending good letters home and postpone or forget to send bad ones.

2 Written lesson plans can never be worth prioritising over real lesson planning that involves thinking and resource preparation. You are only as good as your actual lesson delivery and not your lesson plans. There will only be a few occasions when writing them copiously will be a priority, but you should always do this if you are being inspected. (How else can an outsider discover what you are trying to do in your lesson?) On normal days, write all that is necessary to ensure that you don't forget to do the things you have prepared.

3 Department and pastoral meeting time is built into your regular cycle of non-teaching requirements. Try to influence these so that they include practical activities that will actually help you with lesson planning and curriculum delivery. All too often they become 'moaning' sessions or they are hijacked by senior managers who have their own bureaucratic agendas.

   Nevertheless, meeting time can be a brilliant opportunity to 'chew over ideas' about teaching with colleagues and prepare materials collaboratively. Writing and revising schemes of work as a team is a better way of using limited time than copious marking and individual lesson planning, done in isolation.

4 Some whinging and moaning is a constructive use of departmental time if it is used to let off tension and steam, but it should not be allowed to become the dominant activity.

5 Be smart about marking and assessment; it is often about quality rather than quantity. What does a meticulous A1, B2, C2 in your mark book row after row really mean? Is assessment perhaps better recorded less frequently but as a series of bullet points about

that pupil's overall progress, setting simple targets for improvement rather than having lines of neat marks? Recording marks every time you mark books wastes a lot of precious time to little purpose.

6 In a difficult school is it better to go home early and do no work some evenings rather than get so stressed up about your workload that you spend the next day 'shouting' at the pupils and your colleagues? However, if you always go home within half an hour of the lessons ending, then you are coasting and cutting corners. Teaching is not a nine-to-four job!

7 Pace yourself. You can get more done if things are not left to the last minute. Meet some of your deadlines early to allow you more time to respond to other day-to-day emergencies.

8 Be prepared to say 'no' when someone asks you to do something that will seriously interfere with some basic job of classroom work. If it is a whole school issue, then it might need the involvement of the staff association, department leaders or a union. It is more assertive to say 'no' and give reasons than to say nothing and become stressed. So many teachers manage their time badly, by saying neither 'yes' nor 'no', but passively doing nothing about an issue in the hope that it will simply be forgotten.

9 Most reasonable managers will respond to a sensible 'no' along with some practical reasons for why it has been given. Indeed, truthful feedback is constructive for middle and senior managers as they try to plan improvements in a school.

10 Remember: you will have to do long hours during 'term time' if you work in any school, especially in a 'difficult' one. It is a commitment, and while my 'timing' figures indicate a long working day, the suggestion that you have to juggle priorities still means that you should keep the working day to approximately

8.30am to 5.00pm with a short morning tea break and an average of 25 minutes for lunch. If you are not prepared to do more than office hours during the term, you should not be teaching.

11 It is a fact of professional life that occasional projects may need one or two days' work during the holidays. If you think this is unreasonable you are kidding yourself about the demands of being a successful teacher.

LUNCH AND BREAK DUTIES

There are times when you can find yourself alone and unsupported in tough schools, dealing with some of the set piece spectaculars mentioned in Chapter 11. As a classroom teacher you are contractually liable to do break-duties, but you are entitled to a full one-hour lunch break, without interruption.

As a teacher these duties are best used as a chance to have one-to-one informal chats with the pupils. It is an excellent way of discovering a friendly positive side to pupils who are 'maniacs' in the classroom. As with all things in difficult schools, where you might see someone climbing on a roof to get a ball or dropping litter, try to handle it without having a painful confrontation in which you may be publicly abused. You don't want to create situations out of duties in which you need to follow up incidents. You will have enough of those when teaching in the classrooms.

COVER

You may be asked to cover an absent colleague's lesson about once a week, or maybe more often in periods of crisis. This duty cuts into your non-contact time which has been set aside for other vital tasks. Cover is 'double trouble'. Not only does it stop you doing others things, but it can also lead to fresh confrontations and disciplinary breaches that need to be followed up.

As a general rule it is practical to adhere to the 'art of the possible' when doing it. If you know a class is likely to behave well, then push the cover work and try to get them to do it quietly, even silently. If you know you have an unruly group, then give them the work but don't stress yourself asking them to do it. You will probably have a difficult enough time persuading them to come in and sit down. If this is the case, then let them talk, but don't press too hard on work or you will expend all the patience and energy you will need for one of your own classes later in the day.

Teachers who don't leave any work make your 'cover' really difficult. People who leave you lessons where you have to set up group work or do difficult oral work are also 'taking the mick'. Conserve your energy in covers; the last thing you want to do in these situations is to try to teach. The aim is to supervise the class in the lightest possible way while preparing some of your own work.

Making the most of a cover

Here are things you might be able to do in a cover lesson in a difficult school.

1 Marking, of the scanning and checking variety, rather than assessment which requires careful reading and concentration.
2 Very basic administrative work, such as form filling or memo writing.
3 Filling in 'pro-forma' letters about attendance, punctuality and rewards.
4 Adding up running totals on registers.
5 Talking to pupils, whom you might be teaching later, about their progress in your lesson.

Leaving 'cover work' yourself

1 Set very easy work. Simple questions or note-taking, as self-explanatory as possible. You colleagues will want

to be doing their own work with as little disturbance as possible.

2 Set enough work to keep the keen pupils busy for the whole period.

3 Leave a register for the covered colleague to complete: basic equipment such as exercise books, paper, chalk or dry marker – everything that is needed to make that teacher 'functional' as quickly as possible.

4 Leave clear instructions about what to hand out and collect in from each class – preferably in the format used by all the teachers in the school when out of one of their lessons.

5 Stick it to the desk to ensure that it cannot get lost easily. Better still, leave a spare copy with the deputy responsible for cover or your head of department.

6 It is much better to leave equipment and resources on the teacher's desk than in the usual cupboard or drawer where they cannot be seen. Many classes will disclaim knowledge of this common information about where things are kept in their eagerness to avoid doing any work.

7 Don't let pupils do 'finishing off' work unless you leave very explicit instructions of what it is they have to finish, alongside the materials they were using to do it.

8 Be realistic. Despite what the school policies might say about an absent teachers' responsibility to set work, it becomes very difficult and meaningless after missing a few classes in succession with one particular group. Heads of department in conjunction with hired supply teachers must help you in this situation.

9 Don't waste your best materials on cover lessons when you are 'off'. The likelihood is that the material will not be explained properly or done thoroughly. Save it for when you are in attendance and ready to teach it.

10 If you are going to be absent for a few weeks, then a regular supply teacher should take your lessons. He or she will be trying to teach the material as a regular stand in for you, rather than execute a holding exercise for one lesson while doing their own work like your regular colleagues. They should be using the schemes of work and liaising with your curriculum line manager.

EXTRA-CURRICULAR ACTIVITIES

You will be asked to offer lunchtime or after-school activities in 'difficult' schools. You will probably be more exhausted by your own teaching experiences than the majority of colleagues in secondary education, who don't have to struggle and battle with almost every class they teach.

Advantages of extra-curricular work

1 It is a brilliant way of getting to know a lot of the pupils better as individuals. In rowdy, restless classes you hardly have time to give sane individuals any attention.
2 You can gain the respect of difficult pupils out of the classroom and encourage a much better relationship when you return to the 'classroom trenches'. A one-to-one discussion often works wonders in a difficult school.
3 You can use the threat of withdrawing extra-curricular activity as an 'in-class carrot'.
4 You can offer an activity that extends or enriches a part of the curriculum you are covering in class, or are failing to cover adequately owing to endless disruption.
5 You can offer something completely different to your normal teaching skills and see a different and very positive side to individuals that you didn't believe existed.

6 Like break or lunch duties, it gives you the one-to-one situation and a social edge.

The disadvantages of extra-curricular work

1 You may be interested in some activity, but it is very difficult to get pupils to attend. This can reinforce your frustration and feelings of negativity about the general attitude of your students.
2 Poor and irregular attendance will spoil the momentum of your extra-curricular activity and the enthusiasm you can give it as a teacher.
3 Extra-curricular work eats into precious time when you should be marking books, preparing lessons, seeing parents, or following up your rewards and sanctions.

Chapter 14

Promotion and appeasement in a difficult school

It has already been stated that good relations between you and your middle/senior managers is a key to practical survival in difficult schools. This may not be easy to achieve where tension and stress rise from the need to consume your own classroom smoke and where the high volume of confrontation with pupils is stretching every level of the teaching and management structure. However, progress up the ladder can only happen if you maintain good relations with those who have managerial roles – especially at the highest level.

PROMOTION: THE CONTEXT

1 If you are competent with pupils and meet your deadlines, you have proved yourself. Those who can survive successfully in a difficult class have already demonstrated many leadership qualities.

2 An effective classroom teacher is a commodity that sensible management in a tough school will want to retain at all costs. Few teachers can do it successfully and most want to move on to more amenable educational environments as quickly as possible.

3 Difficult schools have regular turnovers of staff. They often find it difficult to find permanent recruits for the important classroom positions, and are forced to rely on a series of temporary appointments. At one level they are content to make temporary appointments as that gives them the opportunity to circumvent normal selection procedures and discover if the appointee can really handle the pupils in the classroom. Sometimes they simply have to tolerate a 'hand to mouth' staffing situation for certain subjects.

4 They will seek to entice you into staying if you are doing well in the classroom. One of the most practical ways of doing this is to offer you temporary or permanent promotion. Temporary opportunities will be very useful as they will be exchangeable for a permanent promotion in another school. One advantage is that some staff can rise very quickly from rags to riches in a difficult school. They can enter as a supply teacher and achieve a rapid rise into management.

5 It is often useful for CV purposes to work in a difficult school then move to a school in the main stream. Normal schools usually recognise that teachers who have been in the 'front line' have learned some very sharp teaching and management skills through their 'heightened' experience of difficulty.

6 Don't remain too long in a very tough school if you want to fulfil your promotional expectations. After five years you might find that you are too entrenched in the daily experience of the battleground and cannot transfer your competences and skills effectively. You can become 'de-sensitised' to the main stream.

7 Take any promotional experience that is offered to you on a temporary or permanent basis. At the very least it can give you a different perspective of the school and the pupils with whom you are working.

8 Remember that you will only receive promotional offers if you keep constructive relationships with your middle and senior managers. There is little point in being a first-class teacher if you quarrel with all the adults in the institution who are capable of influencing a head's decision to offer you responsibility and opportunity.

FORGIVING, FORGETTING AND APOLOGISING

One of the most important skills to learn in a tough school is the capacity to forgive and forget. It is an art that is needed full time with the pupils if a teacher is to survive and prosper. Yet it is just as important to do the same thing from the head teacher downwards. You must never forget that difficult schools are often set up in 'no-win' situations that put all the staff who work in them under continual pressure and strain. Tempers flare and sharp words are spoken when staff are working under continuous pressure and the worst thing for all concerned is to harbour grudges and sulk. Obviously you cannot control the behaviour of others towards you after a difficult situation has taken place, but, as a general rule, it is always best to try to find a more relaxed moment to reconciliate with that person if possible. In this respect, the most useful tool in your armoury is the capacity to make the first move and apologise. In the frequently macho world of tough schools many pupils and some teachers might see this as a sign of weakness, but it is one of the most assertive ways of disarming a tense situation. I recommend it as a key underpinning strategy to everything you try to do with all the staff you encounter in a difficult school.

There are many teachers who work in difficult schools out of a strong spirit of vocational commitment to improving the opportunities of inner-city pupils. There is genuine reward in having 'success' in the most difficult of environments, but the zeal and dedication of even these committed individuals is being put under strain by the 'blame the teacher' syndrome that has been at the forefront of so many political and media attacks on so-called 'failing' schools. The current climate is demoralising many very dedicated staff in its attempts to weed out a tiny minority of incompetent, lazy or malicious teachers, and there is a general feeling that, irrespective of what you do, it will not be enough.

Chapter 15

Concluding comments

The pressures of unrealistic expectations from mainstream schools is making survival in a difficult school ever more difficult. Teachers are increasingly blamed for the more complex failures of the educational system, with its inappropriate curriculum, its failure to compensate for harsh home backgrounds of pupils with low levels of literacy and numeracy. Teachers are increasingly squeezed. Being asked to be more accountable for the professional task they do is not necessarily a bad thing, but being asked to take the lion's share of the blame for complex failures of the system, in which they are only one group of the many stakeholders, is blatantly unfair.

If you are in a tough school, your performance is going to be scrutinised constantly by outsiders. This may be a tremendous strain, but it is one you will have to learn to tolerate. You have a duty to do your level best for your pupils; they need that commitment from you. That inevitably means questioning, and trying to improve, your own performance. There is, however, a fine line between straining to be more efficient and effective and trying to do the impossible. You can only pray that you have sensible, realistic and hardworking middle and senior managers who take a practical rather than a bureaucratic approach towards improving the teaching and learning in your school.

Difficult schools require not only very committed teachers but also better resources, smaller classes, massive programmes on literacy and numeracy and realistic targets for the improvement of learning and levels of punctuality and attendance. The current inspection system constantly underestimates how difficult good pupil–teacher relations are to achieve in such schools. When it sees them, it is often disappointed by the pace and rigour of the learning that goes with them. But they fail to appreciate the compromises between confrontation and 'forward learning propulsion' that teachers have had to make to obtain a positive atmosphere in many classrooms. These compromises are often interpreted as inadequate teaching and low expectations.

You, the classroom teacher, must look for ways of improving, but within the framework of what you have to react to during your working day. It is by being practical and realistic that you can survive and succeed. It is by taking small, sensible steps that you can improve the quality of education for your pupils, while at the same time responding as sympathetically as you can to the agendas of the politicians and the educational bureaucracy.

Surviving in a difficult school is similar to surviving life as a foot-soldier in the First World War trenches where the strategists, ten miles from the front, have an unrealistic grand plan for winning the war. There will always be a credibility gap between those who have to teach in difficult schools and those who design blue-prints for improvement. Ultimately, both sides need to build up constructive relationships if they are not to pull in different, antagonistic, counter-productive directions.

However, in terms of daily survival, your baseline goal as a teacher is to establish good relationships with the vast majority of pupils, their parents, your colleagues and the various levels of school management.